WOK
AND STIR-FRY DISHES

THE BOOK OF

WOK
AND STIR-FRY DISHES

ELIZABETH WOLF-COHEN

Photographed by
KEN FIELD

a *Salamander book*
Published by Salamander Books Limited
LONDON

Published 1994 by Salamander Books Limited
129-137 York Way, London N7 9LG, United Kingdom

© Salamander Books Ltd 1994

ISBN 0-86101-756-0

Distributed by Hodder & Stoughton Services, PO Box 6,
Mill Road, Dunton Green, Sevenoaks, Kent TN13 2XX

Managing Editor: Felicity Jackson
Art Director: Roger Daniels
Editor: Susan Conder
Photographer: Ken Field, assisted by Teresa Hayhurst
Home Economists: Kerenza Harries and Jo Craig
Typeset by: BMD Graphics, Hemel Hempstead
Colour separation by: Scantrans Pte. Ltd, Singapore
Printed in Belgium by Proost International Book Production

Notes:
All spoon measurements are equal.
1 teaspoon = 5 ml spoon
1 tablespoon = 15 ml spoon.

CONTENTS

COMPANION VOLUMES OF INTEREST:

INTRODUCTION

The wok is one of the most versatile pieces of kitchen equipment, it's quick to use, easy to take care of, and perfect for cooking everything from meat, fish and vegetables to pasta and fruit.

Although it's been in use for thousands of years in China, the wok is still ideal for modern cooking with its emphasis on healthy eating. In a wok, food is cooked quickly and lightly at a very high temperature. This seals in all the flavour and helps to retain the texture and colour as well as essential nutrients.

This book has over 100 delicious recipes for cooking in the wok, including ones for fish, poultry, meat, vegetables, fruit, pasta, rice and noodles. Each recipe is illustrated in full colour and with step-by-step instructions, making this the perfect book for anyone who enjoys good food fast and with the minimum of fuss.

COOKING IN A WOK

The wok was probably invented by the ancient Chinese as a response to constant fuel shortage. It is still the all-purpose cooking utensil in Southeast Asia, but the recent popularity of regional Chinese, Thai, Vietnamese, and Malay cuisines has made it indispensable in Western kitchens as well. The wok's round bottom and high sloping sides conduct heat more evenly than other cookware, so food stirred over a high heat cooks quickly, retaining bright colour, fresh flavour, vitamins and nutrients. This quick-cooking method is also economical. Although lean, tender cuts of meat are required, a little goes a long way, as they are often cooked with several vegetables. Because a very small amount of oil or fat is required, stir-fried food is generally low in fat, cholesterol and calories.

Although stir-frying is quick and easy, preparation of ingredients is very important and every one must be prepared before cooking begins. To ensure food cooks quickly and evenly, cut or chop all ingredients into relatively small, evenly shaped pieces.

CHOOSING A WOK

The traditional, inexpensive Chinese wok is probably still best. Carbon steel, the best conductor of heat, is a better choice than stainless steel, a poor conductor which may scorch and may not withstand very high temperatures. Non-stick woks can be generally useful and less oil or fat is necessary than with a traditional wok. However, they cannot be seasoned like a carbon steel wok and they must not be overheated. Electric woks cannot be used for authentic stir-frying as they do not heat to a high enough temperature and are too shallow.

The Cantonese wok has a short handle on either side and is used especially for steaming and deep-frying. The more round-bottomed Pau wok has one long handle, usually wooden, which does not get hot, so you can hold the wok with one hand, and stir with the other.

Seasoning the Wok: 'Authentic' carbon steel Chinese woks must be 'seasoned' before use and scrubbed to remove protective coating of machine oil applied during manufacturing. To remove this sometimes thick, sticky oil, scrub the wok vigorously with kitchen cleanser and hot water. This is the only time you should scrub the wok, unless it rusts during storage. Dry the wok and place it over a low heat for a few minutes, to dry thoroughly. To season, add 2 tablespoons vegetable oil and, using a double thickness of folded, absorbent kitchen paper, rub a thin film of oil all over the inside of the wok. Heat the wok for a few more minutes and wipe again. The paper will probably be black from machine oil residue. Repeat until the paper stays clean. The wok is now ready for use.

Cleaning the Wok: Food rarely sticks to a seasoned wok, so an ordinary wash in hot water with *no* detergent should suffice. If any food has stuck, use a bamboo wok brush, or ordinary plastic kitchen scrubber. Dry the wok thoroughly and put it over a low heat to prevent rust during storage. As a precaution, rub the inside surface of the dry wok with 1 teaspoon of oil. If the wok rusts, repeat the seasoning process.

CUTTING AND SLICING TECHNIQUES

Cutting and slicing Chinese style is an art. The size and shape of ingredients determines cooking time, and there is little time for foods to absorb flavours and seasonings. Therefore, cut vegetables thinly, with as many cut surfaces as possible. Cut meats, fish and poultry generally across the grain, for maximum tenderness.

Slicing: Hold food firmly against a cutting board with one hand and, with a knife, slice the food straight down into thin strips. Hold a cleaver with your index finger extended over the top edge and your thumb on the near side, to guide the cutting edge. Hold the food with the other hand, tucking your fingers under, so the blade rests against your knuckles for safety. For matchstick-thin strips, square off the sides of the prepared vegetable, cut crossways into 5 cm (2 in) lengths. Stack a few slices and cut even lengthwise strips.

Shredding: Foods such as cabbage or spinach are easily shredded by piling up a few leaves and cutting lengthwise into thin, fine shreds. Roll large leaves, Swiss-roll fashion, before cutting, to reduce width. Meat and poultry breasts or cutlets are easier to shred if frozen for about 20 minutes first.

Horizontal Slicing: To cut thick foods into two or more thin pieces to be sliced or shredded, hold the cleaver or knife parallel to the cutting board. Place one hand flat on the food surface and press down while slicing horizontally into the food. Repeat if necessary.

Diagonal Slicing: Most 'long' vegetables such as spring onions, asparagus or courgettes look more attractive and more surface area is exposed for quicker cooking, if sliced on the diagonal. Angle the cleaver or knife and cut.

Roll Cutting: This is like diagonal cutting, but is suitable for larger or tougher, long vegetables, such as celery or large carrots. Make a diagonal slice at one end. Turn the vegetable 180° and make another diagonal slice. Continue until the whole vegetable is cut into triangular pieces about 2.5 cm (1 in) long.

Dicing: Cut food into slices, then into lengthwise sticks. Stack the sticks and cut crosswise into even-sized cubes.

Chopping: First cut the food into long strips, align them and, holding them with one hand, fingers tucked under, cut crosswise with a knife or cleaver. Use a rocking motion, keeping the tip of the knife or cleaver against the cutting board and using the knuckles as a guide.

STIR-FRYING

Probably the most important technique in stir-frying, is pre-heating the wok. This prevents food sticking and absorbing excess oil. Place the wok over a moderate heat and wait a few minutes until the wok is very hot, then add the oil and swirl to quickly coat the bottom and sides.

For recipes that begin by adding the flavouring ingredients, such as garlic, ginger and spring onions to the oil, it should be only moderately hot or these delicate ingredients may burn or become bitter. If, however, the first ingredient added is a meat or hearty vegetable, make the oil very hot, just below smoking point. As other ingredients are added, stir-fry over a high heat by stirring and tossing them with the metal spatula or spoon. Allow meat to rest a minute on one side before stirring, to cook and brown. Keep the food moving from the centre, up and out onto the side. If a sauce to be thickened with cornflour is added to the dish, remove the wok briefly from the heat and push the food away from the centre so the sauce-thickening mixture goes directly to the bottom of the wok; stir vigorously and then continue tossing the ingredients in the sauce.

——— STIR-FRY INGREDIENTS ———

Bamboo Shoots: Young, tender shoots from the base of bamboo shoots, these are crunchy but bland, absorbing stronger flavours. Sold canned.

Bean Curd: Bean curd, or tofu, in Japanese, is nutritious, low-calorie food made from soy beans. Bland, with a soft-cheese texture, it absorbs other flavours. Stir-fry with care as it can disintegrate. 'Silken tofu' has a much softer texture and is mostly used in soups and sauces.

Black Beans: These small, fermented soy beans are very salty. Black bean sauce, in cans or bottles, is a quick, handy substitute.

Bok Choy: Also known as Chinese cabbage, this resembles Swiss chard.

Daikon: A long white, bland root vegetable with a crunchy texture: also called mooli or Japanese white radish.

Fish Sauce: Also called Nuoc Nam and Nam Pla, made from salted, fermented anchovies and used in sauces, stir-fries and as a condiment. The lighter Vietnamese and Thai sauces are best. A little goes a long way. Keeps indefinitely.

Five-Spice Powder: A blend of cinnamon, cloves, star anise, fennel and Szechuan pepper, used in Chinese marinades and sauces. Sold in super-markets and Asian markets.

Galangal: Known as Thai ginger or laos, this is used fresh, minced or sliced, in soups, sauces and stir-fries. Sold in Asian markets.

Ginger Root: This knobby root's sweet spicy flavour is used in oriental soups, stir-fries and in fish dishes. Store in a dark place, but do not refrigerate.

Hoisin Sauce: This sweet-spicy, dark red-brown condiment is used in Chinese marinades, barbecue sauces and stir-fries. Made from soy flour, chillies, garlic, ginger and sugar. Excellent dipping sauce.

Jicama: A sweet, crunchy Mexican root vegetable similar to water chest-nuts. Add to salads and stir-fries. Peel before using.

Lemon Grass: A, long, thin, lemony herb. Bruise the stems, then chop or slice. Grated lemon or lime peel can be used instead.

Noodles:
Bean Thread Also called cellophane noodles, these transparent noodles are made from ground mung beans. Stir into soups or stir-fry with vegetables. Soak in warm water for 5 minutes for general use, but use unsoaked if deep-frying.
Dried Chinese Spaghetti This thin firm noodle cooks quickly: any thin spag-hetti-type noodle can be substituted. Chinese egg noodles are also sold fresh in supermarkets and Asian markets.
Rice Sticks Long, thin, dried noodles made from rice flour, rice sticks can be fried directly in hot oil and increase many times in volume. A good base for any Chinese-style dish.
Soba This spaghetti-size noodle, made from buckwheat flour, is often used in Japanese soups. Ideal for cold noodle salads. Very quick cooking.

Oriental Aubergine: These long, thin aubergines (eggplants) are tastier than large aubergines (eggplants), do not need peeling and do not absorb much oil. Sold in supermarkets and Asian markets.

Oyster Sauce: A thick, brown, bottled sauce with an un-fishy rich, subtle flavour, made from concentrated oysters and soy sauce. Often used in beef and vegetable stir-fry dishes.

Plum Sauce: A thick, sweet Canton-ese condiment made from plums, apricots, garlic, chillies, sugar, vinegar and flavourings. Use as a dip or a base for barbecue sauces.

Radicchio: A small, tight, slightly bitter, red-leaf chicory. Use shredded in stir-fries, risottos or salads. Sold in supermarkets or Italian markets.

Rice Vinegar: Use Japanese rice vinegar, mild and clear, for salad dress-ings, sauces and pickling. Chinese vinegar is not strong enough.

Rice Wine: Made from fermented rice and yeast, this mellow wine is widely used for stir-fry cooking. A dry sherry can be substituted for it.

Sesame Oil: Made from sesame seeds, this has a rich, golden-brown colour and a nutty flavour and aroma. Has a low smoking point and can burn easily. As a seasoning, a teaspoon added to a stir-fry dish just before serving adds a delicious flavour.

Sesame Paste: Also known as tahini, this is made from ground sesame seeds. It is often combined with garlic, oil, lemon juice and seasonings and used as a Middle-Eastern dipping sauce or condiment.

Sesame Seeds: Widely available, these add texture and flavour to stir-fry dishes. Dry-fry in the wok first to bring out flavour, then stir-fry and use as a garnish. Black sesame seeds can be interchanged with white ones – dry-fry them in the same way..

Soy Sauces: This essential Chinese condiment, flavouring and dipping sauce is made from a fermented mixture of soy beans, flour and water. The more delicate Light Soy Sauce is most common. It is salty, but can be diluted with water. Dark Soy Sauce is thicker and sweeter, containing molasses or caramel. Japanese Soy Sauce, shoyu, is always naturally fermented.

Spring Roll Skins: These paper-thin, flour-dough skins are sold as Shanghi wrappers or lumpia skins. They are thinner and fry more crisply than thicker Cantonese egg roll skins. They can be refrozen.

Star Anise: This eight-pointed star-shaped pod has a mild liquorice flavour and is used in marinades.

Szechuan Peppercorns: These aromatic, reddish-brown dried berries have a mildly spicy flavour. Toast in a dry wok or frying pan before grinding to a powder.

Water Chestnuts: A starchy, bland, crunchy tuber. Use raw in salads or add to soups and stir-fries. Widely sold in cans, rinse in cold water or drop briefly into boiling water, then rinse to remove any metallic taste.

Wonton Skins: These smooth, wheat-flour dough wrappers about 7.5 cm (3 in) square are sold fresh and frozen in supermarkets and Asian markets.

Yellow Bean Paste/Sauce: This thick, aromatic, spicy sauce is made from fermented yellow beans, flour and salt; flavours fish, poultry and vegetables.

—————— CREOLE-STYLE FISH ——————

55 ml (2 fl oz/¼ cup) vegetable oil
1 teaspoon paprika
1 teaspoon dried oregano
½ teaspoon ground cumin
½ teaspoon hot chilli powder
¼ teaspoon black pepper
¼ teaspoon hot pepper sauce (or to taste)
800 g (1¾ lb) firm white fish fillets, such as plaice,
    cut into 2.5 cm (1 in) pieces
1 onion, chopped
3 cloves garlic, finely chopped
4 stalks celery, thinly sliced
1 green pepper (capsicum), diced
1 red pepper (capsicum), diced
225 g (8 oz) fresh okra, sliced
400 g (14 oz) can chopped tomatoes

In a shallow dish, combine 2 tablespoons of the oil, paprika, oregano, cumin, chilli powder, black pepper and hot pepper sauce. Add fish pieces and stir gently to coat. Allow to stand for 15 minutes. Heat the wok over high heat until very hot. With a slotted spoon, drain fish pieces and, working in batches, if necessary, add to the wok. Stir-fry gently for 2 minutes until pieces are firm. Remove to a bowl.

Heat remaining oil in the wok and add onion, garlic and celery. Stir-fry for 1-2 minutes until onion begins to soften. Add green and red peppers (capsicums) and okra and stir-fry for 2-3 minutes. Add any remaining marinade and chopped tomatoes. Bring to the boil and simmer for 4-5 minutes until slightly thickened, stirring frequently. Return fish pieces to wok and cook gently for 1 minute to heat through. Serve with rice.

Serves 6.

— SWEET & SOUR SWORDFISH —

3 tablespoons light soy sauce
2 tablespoons dry sherry or rice wine
3 teaspoons wine or cider vinegar
1 tablespoon sugar
2 teaspoons medium chilli sauce or tomato
   ketchup (sauce)
450 g (1 lb) swordfish steaks, 2.5 cm (1 in) thick
3 tablespoons vegetable oil
1 red pepper (capsicum), cut into 2.5 cm (1 in) pieces
1 green pepper (capsicum), cut into 2.5 cm (1 in) pieces
4 spring onions, cut into 5 cm (2 in) pieces
3 teaspoons cornflour, dissolved in 1 tablespoon
   cold water
150 ml (5 fl oz/⅔ cup) fish or chicken stock

In a bowl, combine soy sauce, sherry or rice wine, vinegar, sugar and chilli sauce or tomato ketchup (sauce). Cut swordfish into strips and stir into marinade to coat. Leave to stand for 20 minutes. Heat the wok until very hot but not smoking, add 2 tablespoons vegetable oil and swirl to coat wok. With a slotted spoon, remove fish pieces from the marinade, draining off and reserving as much liquid as possible. Add fish to the wok and stir-fry for 2-3 minutes, until fish is firm. With a slotted spoon, remove fish strips to a bowl.

Add remaining oil to the wok. Add peppers (capsicums) and stir-fry for 2-3 minutes, until peppers begin to soften. Add spring onions and stir-fry for 1 more minute. Stir the cornflour mixture and add the reserved marinade, then stir in the stock until well blended. Pour into the wok and bring to the boil, stirring frequently. Simmer for 1-2 minutes until thickened. Return swordfish to the sauce and stir gently for 1 minute to heat through. Serve with rice and wild rice garnished with chives.

Serves 4.

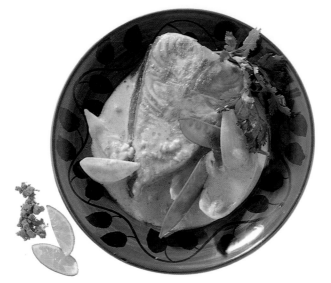

— INDONESIAN-STYLE HALIBUT —

4 halibut fillets, about 175 g (6 oz) each
juice of 1 lime
2 teaspoons ground turmeric
115 ml (4 fl oz/½ cup) vegetable oil
1 clove garlic, finely chopped
1 cm (½ in) piece fresh root ginger, peeled and
    finely chopped
1 fresh chilli, seeded and chopped
1 onion, sliced lengthwise to form 'petals'
2 teaspoons ground coriander
150 ml (5 fl oz/⅔ cup) unsweetened coconut milk
1 teaspoon sugar
½ teaspoon salt
175 g (6 oz) mange tout (snow peas)
fresh coriander sprigs, to garnish

Place fish fillets in a shallow dish. Sprinkle with the lime juice and rub the turmeric into both sides of each fillet. Set aside. In a wok, heat half the oil until hot, but not smoking; swirl to coat wok. Gently slide 2 of the fish fillets into the oil and fry for 4-5 minutes, carefully turning once during cooking. Remove and drain on absorbent kitchen paper. Add remaining oil to wok and fry remaining fish fillets in the same way. Drain as before and keep fish fillets warm.

Pour off all but 1 tablespoon oil from the wok. Add garlic, ginger and chilli and stir-fry for 1 minute. Add the onion 'petals' and coriander and stir-fry for 2 minutes until onion begins to soften. Stir in coconut milk, sugar and salt and bring to the boil, adding a little more water if sauce is too thick. Stir in the mange tout (snow peas) and cook for 1 minute, until they turn bright green. Spoon sauce over fish fillets and garnish with fresh coriander. Serve immediately.

Serves 4.

—— BLACKENED TUNA PIECES ——

1 teaspoon chilli powder (or to taste)
½ teaspoon ground black pepper
1 teaspoon ground coriander
½ teaspoon ground cumin
½ teaspoon ground turmeric
1 teaspoon paprika
½ teaspoon dried thyme
55 ml (2 fl oz/¼ cup) vegetable oil
3 tablespoons orange juice
3 tablespoons cider vinegar
1 tablespoon honey
4 tuna steaks, about 225 g (8 oz) each and 2.5 cm (1 in)
   thick, cut into pieces
2 cloves garlic, finely chopped
4 spring onions, thinly sliced

In a shallow dish, combine chilli powder, black pepper, ground coriander, cumin, turmeric, paprika and thyme. In another shallow dish, combine oil, orange juice, vinegar and honey. Toss tuna pieces in oil mixture to coat all sides, then dip each tuna piece into the spice mixture to coat each side evenly.

Heat dry wok over high heat until very hot. Add tuna pieces and stir-fry for 3-5 minutes until firm. Remove to warm plates. Add oil mixture to wok and stir to deglaze any spice mixture. Add garlic and spring onions and stir-fry for 1-2 minutes. Spoon sauce over tuna and serve with a brown rice pilaf.

Serves 4.

──TUNA, TOMATO & PENNE──

2 tablespoons olive oil
1 onion, chopped
2 cloves garlic, finely chopped
800 g (28 oz) can peeled tomatoes
1 tablespoon tomato purée (paste)
1 tablespoon chopped fresh oregano or 1 teaspoon dried
55 g (2½ oz/⅓ cup) sun-dried tomatoes in oil, drained
   and chopped
salt and fresh ground black pepper
350 g (12 oz) penne or rigatoni
55 g (2½ oz/⅓ cup) black olives, coarsely chopped
2 tablespoons capers, drained
200 g (7 oz) can light tuna, drained
2 tablespoons chopped fresh parsley
Parmesan cheese, to garnish

Heat the wok until hot. Add the oil and swirl to coat wok. Add onion and garlic and stir-fry for 1-2 minutes until beginning to soften. Add the tomatoes, stirring to break up the large pieces. Stir in the tomato purée (paste), oregano and sun-dried tomatoes. Bring to the boil and simmer for 10-12 minutes until sauce is slightly thickened. Season with salt and pepper. Meanwhile, in a large saucepan of boiling water, cook penne according to packet directions.

Stir black olives, capers and tuna into the sauce. Drain pasta and add to sauce, stirring gently to mix well. Stir in chopped parsley and serve immediately from the wok, or spoon into 4 soup plates. Using a swivel-bladed vegetable peeler, shave flakes of Parmesan over each serving. Alternatively, grate Parmesan over each serving.

Serves 4.

—— TUNA WITH SPICY SALSA ——

2 tablespoons sesame oil
1 tablespoon light soy sauce
1 clove garlic, finely chopped
700 g (1 ½ lb) tuna steaks, 2.5 cm (1 in) thick,
   cut into chunks
2 tablespoons vegetable oil
225 g (8 oz) daikon (mooli), peeled and diced
225 g (8 oz) cucumber, peeled, seeded and diced
1 red pepper (capsicum), diced
1 red onion, coarsely chopped
1 fresh chilli, seeded and finely chopped
2 tablespoons lime juice
1 teaspoon sugar
1 tablespoon sesame seeds, toasted
lime wedges and fresh coriander sprigs, to garnish

In a shallow dish, combine 1 tablespoon sesame oil with soy sauce and garlic. Add tuna chunks and toss gently to coat. Allow to stand for 15 minutes. Heat the wok until very hot; add 1 tablespoon of the vegetable oil and swirl to coat. Add daikon, cucumber, red pepper (capsicum), red onion and fresh chilli and stir-fry for 2-3 minutes until vegetables begin to soften and turn a bright colour. Stir in lime juice, sugar and remaining sesame oil and cook for 30 seconds until sugar dissolves. Remove to a bowl.

Add remaining vegetable oil to wok and, working in batches, if necessary, add the fish chunks and stir-fry gently for 2-3 minutes, until firm. Arrange fish on 4 dinner plates and sprinkle with the sesame seeds. Spoon some of the warm relish onto each plate and garnish with lime wedges and fresh coriander sprigs. Serve with noodles.

Serves 4.

— SNAPPER WITH CAPELLINI —

1 tablespoon olive oil
55 g (2 oz/¼ cup) unsalted butter
450 g (1 lb) red snapper or sea bass fillets, cut into
   2.5 cm (1 in) strips
salt and freshly ground black pepper
225 g (8 oz) mushrooms, quartered
2 cloves garlic, finely chopped
150 ml (5 fl oz/⅔ cup) dry white wine
2 tomatoes, peeled, seeded and chopped
juice of 1 lemon
1 tablespoon tomato purée (paste)
4 spring onions, thinly sliced
2 tablespoons thinly shredded fresh basil
450 g (1 lb) capellini or thin spaghetti
fresh basil sprigs, to garnish

Heat the wok until hot. Add oil and swirl to coat wok. Add half the butter and swirl to mix with oil. Add snapper or bass strips and gently stir-fry for 1-2 minutes until just firm. Season with salt and pepper and, with a slotted spoon, remove to a bowl. Stir mushrooms into remaining oil and butter in the wok, then add garlic and stir-fry for 1 minute. Add white wine and stir to deglaze any bits stuck to wok. Bring to the boil and simmer for 1 minute.

Add chopped tomatoes, lemon juice, tomato purée (paste), spring onions and basil, stirring frequently. Whisk in remaining butter in small pieces to thicken and smooth sauce. Return fish to sauce and cook gently for 1 minute until heated through. Meanwhile, in a large saucepan of boiling water, cook capellini or spaghetti according to directions. Drain and divide among 4 plates. Top with fish strips and sauce and garnish with fresh basil sprigs.

Serves 4.

FIVE-SPICE SALMON

1 teaspoon sesame oil
3 tablespoons soy sauce
3 tablespoons dry sherry or rice wine
1 tablespoon honey
1 tablespoon lime or lemon juice
1 teaspoon five-spice powder
700 g (1½ lb) salmon fillet, skinned and cut into
    2.5 cm (1 in) strips
2 egg whites
3 teaspoons cornflour
300 ml (10 fl oz/1¼ cups) vegetable oil
6 spring onions, sliced into 5 cm (2 in) pieces
115 ml (4 fl oz/½ cup) light fish or chicken
    stock or water
dash hot pepper sauce (optional)
lime wedges, to garnish

In a shallow baking dish, combine the sesame oil, soy sauce, sherry or wine, honey, lime or lemon juice and five-spice powder. Add salmon strips and toss gently to coat. Leave to stand for 30 minutes. With a slotted spoon, remove the salmon strips from marinade and pat dry with absorbent kitchen paper. Reserve marinade. In a small dish, beat egg whites and cornflour to make a batter. Add salmon strips and toss gently to coat completely.

Heat the vegetable oil in the wok until hot. Add the salmon in batches. Fry for 2-3 minutes until golden, turning once. Remove and drain on absorbent kitchen paper. Pour oil from wok and wipe wok clean. Pour marinade into wok and add spring onions, stock or water and pepper sauce, if using. Bring to the boil and simmer for 1-2 minutes. Add fish and turn gently to coat. Cook for 1 minute until hot. Garnish with lime and serve with noodles.

Serves 4.

STEAMED SEA BASS

1 kg (2¼ lb) sea bass, gutted, with head and
    tail left on
1 tablespoon Japanese rice wine or dry sherry
1 teaspoon sea salt
1 tablespoon peanut oil
2 tablespoons fermented black beans, rinsed, drained
    and coarsely chopped
1 clove garlic, finely chopped
1 cm (½ in) piece fresh root ginger, peeled and
    finely chopped
3 spring onions, thinly sliced
2 tablespoons soy sauce
115 ml (4 fl oz/½ cup) fish or chicken stock
6 teaspoons mild Chinese chilli sauce
1 teaspoon sesame oil
fresh coriander or spring onions, to garnish

With a sharp knife, make 3 or 4 diagonal
slashes 1 cm (½ in) deep on both sides of fish.
Sprinkle inside and out with wine or sherry
and salt. Place in an oval baking dish which
will fit in a wok. Allow to stand 20 minutes.
Place a wire rack or an inverted ramekin and
a plate in wok. Fill wok with 2.5 cm (1 in)
water and bring to the boil. Place dish with
the fish on the rack or ramekins and cover
tightly. Cook for 8-12 minutes, until fish
flakes easily. Remove fish from wok and keep
warm. Remove rack or ramekin and plate and
pour off water. Wipe wok dry and reheat.

Add peanut oil and swirl to coat wok. Add
the black beans, garlic and ginger and stir-fry
for 1 minute. Stir in the spring onions, soy
sauce and stock and bring to the boil; cook for
1 minute. Stir in the chilli sauce and sesame
oil and remove from the heat. Pour sauce
over fish and serve immediately, garnished
with fresh coriander or spring onions.

Serves 4.

——SINGAPORE CHILLI CRAB——

1 tablespoon vegetable oil
1 tablespoon sesame oil
4 cloves garlic, finely chopped
2.5 cm (1 in) fresh root ginger, peeled and chopped
2 tablespoons wine vinegar
150 ml (5 fl oz/²⁄₃ cup) light fish or chicken stock
70 ml (2½ fl oz/¹⁄₃ cup) tomato ketchup (sauce)
3 teaspoons each hot chilli sauce and soy sauce
1 tablespoon brown sugar
2½ teaspoons cornflour dissolved in 3 tablespoons
    water
4 spring onions, thinly sliced
1 large cooked crab, cleaned and in the shell, chopped
    into serving pieces, with legs and claws cracked open,
    or 4 large crab claws, cracked open
cucumber matchsticks and coriander sprigs, to garnish

Heat the wok until very hot. Add the oils and
swirl to coat the wok. Add garlic and ginger
and stir-fry for 1-2 minutes until softened, but
do not brown. Stir in wine vinegar, fish or
chicken stock, tomato ketchup (sauce),
chilli sauce, soy sauce and sugar and bring
to the boil.

Stir the cornflour mixture, and stir into the
wok with spring onions and crab pieces or
claws. Simmer crab pieces in the sauce for
2-4 minutes, until sauce thickens and crab
is heated through. Garnish with cucumber
matchsticks and coriander sprigs and serve
with plain boiled rice.

Serves 4.

CRAB WONTONS

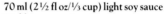

70 ml (2½ fl oz/⅓ cup) light soy sauce
2 tablespoons wine vinegar
2 tablespoons sesame oil
½ teaspoon crushed dried chillies
2 teaspoons honey or sugar
6-8 canned whole water chestnuts, rinsed and minced
2 spring onions, finely chopped
1 teaspoon finely chopped fresh root ginger
225 g (8 oz) white crabmeat, drained and picked over
½ teaspoon red pepper sauce
1 tablespoon finely chopped fresh coriander or dill
1 egg yolk
30 wonton skins
vegetable oil for deep frying

In a small bowl, mix together 55 ml (2 fl oz/¼ cup) soy sauce, wine vinegar, 1 tablespoon sesame oil, 1 tablespoon water, crushed chillies and honey or sugar. Set aside. Heat remaining oil in the wok, add the water chestnuts, spring onions and root ginger and stir-fry for 1-2 minutes. Cool slightly, then mix with crab, remaining soy sauce, red pepper sauce, fresh coriander or dill and egg yolk. Place a teaspoon of mixture in the centre of each wonton skin. Dampen edges with a little water and fold up one corner to opposite corner to form a triangle.

Fold over the bottom 2 corners to meet and press together to resemble a tortelloni. Be sure the filling is well-sealed. In the wok, heat 7.5 cm (3 in) vegetable oil to 190C (375F) and deep fry the wontons in batches for 3 minutes, until golden on all sides, turning once during cooking. Remove with a Chinese strainer or slotted spoon to absorbent kitchen paper to drain. Serve with the dipping sauce and a salad.

Makes 30 wontons.

——— HOT PRAWN SALAD ———

mixed salad leaves for serving
2 mangoes, peeled and sliced
2 tablespoons olive oil
150 g (5 oz) sugar snap peas
4-6 spring onions, thinly sliced into 2.5 cm (1 in) pieces
15 g (½ oz/1 tablespoon) butter
450 g (1 lb) cooked tiger prawns, peeled and deveined
1 tablespoon anise-flavoured liqueur
55 ml (2 fl oz/¼ cup) whipping cream
pinch freshly grated nutmeg
salt and freshly ground black pepper
2 tablespoons chopped fresh dill
fresh dill sprigs, to garnish

Arrange the salad leaves on one side of 4 large plates and fan out the mango slices on the other side; set aside. Heat the oil in the wok and swirl to coat wok. Add sugar snap peas and spring onions and stir fry for 1-2 minutes until beans turn bright green and onions begin to soften. With a strainer or slotted spoon, remove to a bowl.

Add butter to oil in the wok and stir in prawns. Stir-fry for 1-2 minutes until heated through; do not overcook. Remove to the bowl. Pour in anise-flavour liqueur and stir to deglaze the wok. Cook for 1 minute, then stir in cream and bring to the boil. Season with nutmeg, salt and pepper. Stir in dill, prawns, sugar snap peas and spring onions, tossing to coat. Immediately, spoon mixture onto salad leaves and garnish with dill sprigs.

Serves 4.

—— 'MOCK' LOBSTER STIR-FRY ——

15 cm (6 in) stalk fresh lemon grass, trimmed
1 teaspoon tomato purée (paste)
1 tablespoon vegetable oil
1 tablespoon sesame oil
450 g (1 lb) monkfish tails, skinned and cut into
    chunks, or 450 g (1 lb) cooked lobster
3 cloves garlic, finely chopped
2.5 cm (1 in) fresh root ginger, peeled and chopped
1 onion, cut lengthwise into 'petals'
1 fresh chilli, seeded and finely chopped
2 tomatoes, peeled, seeded and chopped
1 teaspoon sugar
2 large spring onions, sliced into 2.5 cm (1 in) pieces
2 tablespoons fresh chopped coriander
1 tablespoon lime juice
lime wedges and coriander, to garnish

Crush lemon grass and cut into 2.5 cm (1 in) pieces. Place in a saucepan with 175 ml (6 fl oz/¾ cup) water and bring to the boil. Simmer for 3 minutes. Add tomato purée (paste); stir until dissolved. Set aside. Heat the oils in the wok until very hot. Add fish and stir-fry for 3-4 minutes, until firm. Transfer fish to a bowl. If using lobster, stir-fry for 1-2 minutes, then transfer to a bowl. Add garlic and ginger to wok and stir-fry for 10 seconds. Add onion and chilli and stir-fry for 1-2 minutes, until onion begins to soften. Add tomatoes, sugar and lemon grass mixture.

Add spring onions, chopped coriander and lime juice; cook for 1 minute until spring onions turn bright green. Return fish or lobster to wok and cook for 1 minute until it is heated through. Serve immediately, garnished with lime wedges and coriander. Accompany with noodles.

Serves 2.

Note: Monkfish (anglerfish) is often called 'poor man's lobster' due to its sweet flavour and firm, lobster-like texture.

– LOBSTER IN MUSTARD CREAM –

450 g (1 lb) new potatoes, cut in half, if large
15 g (½ oz/1 tablespoon) butter
1 onion, finely chopped
1 clove garlic, finely chopped
225 g (8 oz) mushrooms
115 ml (4 fl oz/½ cup) dry white wine
225 ml (8 fl oz/1 cup) double or whipping cream
pinch freshly grated nutmeg
salt and freshly ground black pepper
4 spring onions, thinly sliced
1-2 tablespoons Dijon mustard
450 g (1 lb) cooked lobster meat
225 g (8 oz) peeled cooked prawns, defrosted and dried,
　if frozen
2 tablespoons shredded fresh basil
basil leaves, to garnish

In a saucepan of boiling water, cook new potatoes for 12-15 minutes until tender when pierced with a sharp knife. Heat the wok until hot. Add butter and swirl to melt and coat wok. Add onion and garlic and stir-fry for 1 minute. Add mushrooms and stir-fry for a further 1-2 minutes. Add white wine and bring to the boil. Simmer for 2-3 minutes until reduced by half. Stir in the cream and bring back to the boil. Simmer for 5-6 minutes until reduced and thickened. Season with nutmeg, salt and freshly ground pepper and stir in spring onions.

Stir in 1 tablespoon Dijon mustard, lobster and prawns and cook 1-2 minutes. Add chopped basil and new potatoes. Taste and stir in remaining mustard for a stronger flavour. Spoon onto dinner plates and garnish with fresh basil leaves.

Serves 4.

Variation: Cooked prawns can be substituted for the lobster meat. Alternatively, 700 g (1½ lb) cooked monkfish (anglerfish) pieces can be substituted for the lobster and prawns.

—CHILLI CUCUMBER PRAWNS—

450 g (1 lb) cooked prawns, in the shell
1 tablespoon vegetable oil
1 tablespoon sesame oil
2.5 cm (1 in) piece fresh root ginger, peeled and
    finely chopped
2-3 cloves garlic, finely minced
2-3 fresh chillies, seeded and chopped (or to taste)
½ cucumber, peeled, seeded and diced
2-3 spring onions, thinly sliced
2 tablespoons tomato ketchup (sauce)
3 teaspoons wine vinegar
½ teaspoon sugar

Using kitchen scissors or small sharp knife, cut along backs of prawn shell to expose the black vein. Keeping shells intact, rinse out the vein under running cold water. Pat prawns dry with absorbent kitchen paper. Heat the wok until hot. Add oils, swirling to coat wok. Add ginger, garlic and chillies and stir-fry for 1 minute until very fragrant but not brown. Increase heat and add the prawns. Stir-fry for 1-2 minutes until prawns are hot.

Stir in the cucumber and spring onions. Add the tomato ketchup (sauce), wine vinegar and sugar and stir-fry for 1 minute, until prawns are lightly coated with sauce and cucumber looks translucent. Serve the prawns immediately.

Serves 2.

—JASMINE-SCENTED PRAWNS—

3 tablespoons Japanese rice wine, sake or dry sherry
1 tablespoon light soy sauce
2.5 cm (1 in) piece fresh root ginger, peeled and
   finely chopped
1 teaspoon sesame oil
¼ teaspoon salt
700 g (1½ lb) raw medium prawns, shelled and
   deveined, tails left on if wished
2 tablespoons jasmine or other aromatic tea leaves,
   such as Earl Grey
115 ml (4 fl oz/½ cup) light fish or chicken stock
2 teaspoons cornflour, dissolved in 1 tablespoon water
½ teaspoon sugar
1 tablespoon vegetable oil
4 spring onions, thinly sliced
mint sprigs or jasmine flowers, to garnish

In a medium bowl, combine rice wine, sake
or dry sherry, soy sauce, ginger, sesame oil
and salt. Add prawns and toss to coat well.
Allow to stand for 30 minutes, stirring once
or twice. In a small bowl, stir the tea leaves
into 115 ml (4 fl oz/½ cup) boiling water and
allow to steep for 1 minute. Strain tea
through a fine tea strainer or sieve into
another bowl and discard the tea leaves. Add
the fish or chicken stock to the tea and stir in
the cornflour mixture and sugar.

Heat wok until hot, add vegetable oil and
swirl to coat wok. With a Chinese strainer or
slotted spoon, remove prawns from marinade. Working in batches, add prawns to
wok and stir-fry for 1-2 minutes until pink
and firm; remove to a bowl. Stir in spring
onions and reserved marinade and cook for
1 minute. Stir tea mixture and add to wok,
stirring until thickened. Return prawns to
wok and toss lightly to coat. Garnish with
mint or jasmine and serve with rice.

Serves 4.

PACIFIC PRAWNS

2 tablespoons peanut oil
450 g (1 lb) raw medium prawns, shelled and deveined
2 cloves garlic, finely chopped
2.5 cm (1 in) piece fresh root ginger, peeled and
    finely chopped
2 stalks celery, sliced
1 red pepper (capsicum), sliced
4 spring onions, cut into thin strips
225 g (8 oz) can unsweetened pineapple chunks,
    drained, juice reserved
2 teaspoons cornflour
2 teaspoons soy sauce
1 tablespoon lemon juice
dash hot pepper sauce
150 g (5oz/1 cup) macadamia nuts, rinsed
    lightly if salted

Heat the wok until hot. Add 1 tablespoon oil
and swirl to coat wok. Add prawns and stir-
fry for 2 minutes until prawns turn pink and
feel firm to the touch. Remove to bowl. Add
remaining oil to the wok. Add garlic and
ginger and stir-fry for 30 seconds. Stir in
celery, red pepper (capsicum) and spring
onions and stir-fry for 3-4 minutes until
vegetables are tender but still crisp. Stir in
pineapple chunks.

Dissolve the cornflour in the reserved pineapple juice. Stir in the soy sauce, lemon juice
and hot pepper sauce. Stir into the vegetable
and pineapple mixture and bring to simmering point. Add reserved prawns and macadamia nuts and stir-fry until sauce thickens and
prawns are heated through.

Serves 4.

— PRAWNS WITH RADICCHIO —

2 tablespoons olive oil
4 cloves garlic, finely chopped
2 shallots, finely chopped
4 slices bacon, diced
700 g (1½ lb) raw medium prawns,
   shelled and deveined
115 ml (4 fl oz/½ cup) grappa or brandy
225 g (8 oz) radicchio, thinly shredded
250 ml (9 fl oz/1 cup) whipping cream
salt and freshly ground black pepper
3-4 tablespoons chopped fresh parsley
450 g (1 lb) linguine

Heat wok until hot. Add olive oil and swirl to coat wok. Add garlic, shallots and bacon.

Stir-fry for 1-2 minutes until bacon is crisp. Add prawns and stir-fry for 2 minutes until prawns turn pink and feel firm to the touch. With a Chinese strainer or slotted spoon, remove prawns to a bowl. Add grappa or brandy and bring to the boil, stirring frequently. Stir in shredded radicchio, cream, salt and pepper and bring to simmering point; cook for 1 minute until sauce thickens slightly. Return prawns to wok and stir to coat. Stir in half the parsley.

In a large saucepan of boiling water, cook the linguine according to packet directions. Drain and divide among 4 large bowls. Spoon prawns and sauce equally over pasta and sprinkle with remaining parsley.

Serves 4.

Variation: Cooked prawns can be substituted; but do not stir-fry. Add to thickened sauce and heat through gently for 1 minute before adding parsley.

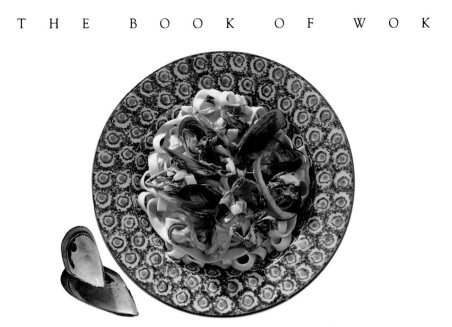

— MUSSELS WITH WATERCRESS —

36-40 large mussels
2 tablespoons olive oil
1 onion, finely chopped
2 cloves garlic, finely chopped
250 ml (9 fl oz/1 cup) light fish or chicken stock
1 small red pepper (capsicum), thinly sliced
150 ml (5 fl oz/²⁄₃ cup) whipping cream
2 bunches watercress or rocket, washed,
   dried and chopped
salt and freshly ground pepper
450 g (1 lb) tagliatelle

With a stiff brush, scrub mussels. Discard any that are not tightly closed. Using a small knife, remove beards and barnacles.

Heat the wok until hot. Add the olive oil and swirl to coat wok. Add the onion and garlic and stir-fry for 1-2 minutes, until onion begins to soften. Stir in the fish or chicken stock and the mussels. Bring to the boil, cover and simmer for 3-4 minutes until mussels open. Using a Chinese strainer, scoop out the mussels into a large bowl; discard any unopened mussels. If you like, remove and discard half the mussel shells.

Add the red pepper (capsicum) and boil the cooking liquid until reduced to about 250 ml (9 fl oz/1 cup). Add cream and simmer for a further 3 minutes until slightly thickened. Stir in the watercress or rocket and season with salt and pepper. Return the mussels to the sauce, stirring to heat through. In a large saucepan of boiling water, cook the tagliatelle according to the packet directions. Drain and divide among 4 soup plates. Top with equal amounts of mussels and sauce.

Serves 4.

————OYSTER WOK STEW————

olive oil for frying
1 small loaf French or Italian bread, cut into 1 cm
  (½ in) cubes
freshly ground black pepper
Parmesan cheese for sprinkling
15 g (½ oz/1 tablespoon) butter
1 small onion, finely chopped
1 clove garlic, finely minced
2 tablespoons flour
400 g (14 oz) can chopped tomatoes, drained
½ teaspoon chilli powder or hot pepper sauce to taste
½ teaspoon paprika
24-30 shucked oysters, liquid reserved
450 ml (16 fl oz/2 cups) whipping cream
250 ml (9 fl oz/1 cup) milk
2 tablespoons chopped fresh parsley

Heat 5 cm (2 in) oil in the wok until very hot,
but not smoking. Add bread cubes and,
working in batches, deep-fry for 1 minute
until golden. Drain on absorbent kitchen
paper, then sprinkle with pepper and
Parmesan cheese, tossing to coat. Pour off all
but 1 tablespoon oil and return wok to heat.
Add the butter, onion and garlic and stir-fry
for 1-2 minutes until onion begins to soften.
Add flour and cook for 1 minute. Add tomatoes, chilli powder or hot pepper sauce and
paprika and cook for 3-4 minutes until thickened, stirring frequently.

Through a muslin-lined strainer, pour in the
reserved oyster liquid. Stir in the whipping
cream and milk and slowly bring to simmering point. Cook for 4-5 minutes until sauce
thickens and reduces slightly. Season with
black pepper. Add oysters to liquid and simmer gently for 1-2 minutes until edges of the
oysters begin to curl. Stir in chopped parsley
and pour into soup plates. If you like, sprinkle
with extra Parmesan and pass croûtons
separately.

Serves 4-6.

──── MALAY CURRIED CLAMS ────

24 steamer (soft-shell) clams
1 tablespoon vegetable oil
1 tablespoon sesame oil
2 cloves garlic, finely chopped
2.5 cm (1 in) piece fresh root ginger, peeled and
    finely chopped
1 tablespoon fermented black beans, rinsed and
    chopped
3 teaspoons curry paste or 6 teaspoons curry powder
250 ml (9 fl oz/1 cup) light fish or chicken stock
55 ml (2 fl oz/¼ cup) tomato ketchup (sauce)
2 tablespoons oyster sauce
1 tablespoon soy sauce
1 teaspoon Chinese chilli sauce
2 teaspoons cornflour dissolved in 3 tablespoons water
4 spring onions, thinly sliced

With stiff brush, scrub clams well. Cover with cold water and soak for about 1 hour. With a Chinese strainer, carefully remove clams from soaking liquid to a colander. (This leaves any sand or grit on the bottom.) Discard any clams that are not tightly closed. Heat oils in the wok, swirling to mix oils and coat wok. Add garlic, ginger and black beans and stir-fry for 30 seconds until fragrant. Stir in curry paste or powder and cook for 1 minute, stirring constantly.

Stir in clams, fish or chicken stock, tomato ketchup (sauce), oyster sauce, soy sauce and chilli sauce. Bring to the boil, cover and simmer for about 5 minutes until clams open. Stir cornflour mixture and stir into clams with spring onions. Stir until sauce thickens and spring onions turn a bright colour. Discard any unopened clams. Serve immediately with steamed rice or noodles.

Serves 2.

—— SWEET & SOUR SCALLOPS ——

15 cm (6 in) stalk fresh lemon grass, trimmed
2 tablespoons peanut oil
2 cloves garlic, finely chopped
2.5 cm (1 in) piece fresh root ginger, peeled and
    finely chopped
1 fresh chilli, seeded and chopped
450 g (1 lb) sea scallops, cut in half crosswise
1 green pepper (capsicum), diced
1 red pepper (capsicum), diced
4-6 spring onions, thinly sliced
70 ml (2½ fl oz/⅓ cup) seasoned rice vinegar
2-3 tablespoons nam pla (Thai fish sauce)
1 teaspoon sugar
1 tomato, peeled, seeded and chopped
3 tablespoons chopped fresh coriander, plus sprigs
    for garnishing

Crush lemon grass stalk and cut into 1 cm
(½ in) pieces. Heat the wok until hot, add
the oil and swirl to coat wok. Add lemon
grass, garlic, ginger and chilli and stir-fry for
30 seconds. Add scallops and stir-fry for
3 minutes until they are opaque and slightly
firm to the touch. With a Chinese strainer or
slotted spoon, remove to a bowl.

Add green and red peppers (capsicums) and
spring onions to the wok and stir-fry for 2-3
minutes until vegetables begin to soften. Add
vinegar, nam pla, sugar, tomato and chopped
coriander. Return scallops to the wok and
toss for 30-50 seconds to coat with the sauce
and heat through. Garnish with coriander
sprigs and serve with boiled and wild rice.

Serves 4.

—SCALLOPS WITH CASHEWS—

55 ml (2 fl oz/¼ cup) dry sherry or rice wine
3 tablespoons tomato ketchup (sauce)
1 tablespoon oyster sauce
1 tablespoon wine vinegar
1 tablespoon sesame oil
1 teaspoon Chinese chilli sauce (or to taste)
1 tablespoon grated orange zest and 1 tablespoon
    orange juice
1 teaspoon cornflour
1 tablespoon vegetable oil
700 g (1 ½ lb) queen scallops
2 cloves garlic, finely chopped
4 spring onions, thinly sliced
175 g (6 oz) fresh asparagus, cut into 2.5 cm
    (1 in) pieces
150 g (5 oz) cashew nuts, lightly rinsed

In a medium bowl, combine dry sherry or rice wine, tomato ketchup (sauce), oyster sauce, wine vinegar, sesame oil, chilli sauce, orange zest and juice and cornflour. Heat the wok until hot, add oil and swirl to coat wok. Add scallops and stir-fry for 1-2 minutes until they begin to turn opaque. Remove to a bowl.

Add garlic, spring onions and asparagus and stir-fry for 2-3 minutes, until asparagus is bright green and tender but still crisp. Stir sauce ingredients and pour into the wok. Bring to simmering point. Return scallops to the wok and add the cashews. Stir-fry for 1 minute until scallops are heated through, tossing to coat all ingredients. Serve with rice garnished with strips of orange rind.

Serves 4.

—— THAI CURRIED SEAFOOD ——

2 tablespoons vegetable oil
450 g (1 lb) sea scallops, cut in half lengthwise
1 onion, chopped
5 cm (2 in) piece fresh root ginger, peeled and finely
    chopped
4 cloves garlic, finely chopped
3 teaspoons curry paste or 6 teaspoons curry powder
1½ teaspoons each ground coriander and cumin
15 cm (6 in) stalk lemon grass, crushed
225 g (8 oz) can chopped tomatoes
115 ml (4 fl oz/½ cup) chicken stock
450 ml (16 fl oz/2 cups) unsweetened coconut milk
12 mussels, scrubbed and debearded
450 g (1 lb) cooked, peeled prawns, deveined
12 crab sticks, defrosted and dried if frozen
chopped fresh coriander and shaved coconut, to garnish

Heat the wok until hot and add 1 tablespoon
oil; swirl to coat wok. Add scallops and stir-
fry for 2-3 minutes until opaque and firm.
Remove to bowl. Add remaining oil to the
wok and add onion, ginger and garlic. Stir-fry
for 1-2 minutes until onion begins to soften.
Add curry paste or powder, coriander, cumin
and lemon grass. Stir-fry for 1-2 minutes.
Add the canned tomatoes and the stock.
Bring to the boil, stirring frequently. Simmer
for 5 minutes until slightly reduced and
thickened. Add the coconut milk and
simmer for 2-3 minutes.

Stir mussels into sauce and cook, covered, for
1-2 minutes, until mussels begin to open. Stir
in prawns, crab sticks cut into 1 cm (½ in)
pieces, and reserved scallops. Cook, covered,
1-2 minutes more until all mussels open and
seafood is heated through. Remove the
lemon grass stalk and discard any mussels
that have not opened. Serve garnished with
chopped coriander and shaved coconut.
Serve with steamed rice.

Serves 6-8.

—— SEAFOOD JAMBALAYA ——

2 tablespoons vegetable oil
450 g (1 lb) raw medium prawns, shelled and deveined
225 g (8 oz) sea scallops
225 g (8 oz) pork sausage meat
1 tablespoon flour
1 large onion, chopped
3 cloves garlic, chopped
2 stalks celery, thinly sliced
1 green and 1 red pepper (capsicum), diced
3 teaspoons Cajun seasoning mix or chilli powder
350 g (12 oz/1½ cups) long-grain rice
400 g (14 oz) can chopped tomatoes
450 ml (16 fl oz/2 cups) chicken stock
salt and freshly ground black pepper
450 g (1 lb) cooked crayfish tails or meat from 1 crab
chopped fresh parsley, to garnish

Heat wok until hot, add oil and swirl to coat wok. Add prawns and stir-fry for 2-3 minutes, until prawns turn pink and feel firm to touch. Remove to a bowl. Add scallops to wok and stir-fry for 2-3 minutes until opaque and firm. Remove scallops to bowl. Stir sausage meat into wok and stir-fry for 4-5 minutes, until well browned. Stir flour into sausage meat until completely blended, then add onion, garlic, celery, peppers (capsicums) and Cajun seasoning mix or chilli powder. Stir-fry for 4-5 minutes until vegetables begin to soften, then stir in rice.

Add chopped tomatoes with their liquid and chicken stock; stir well and season with salt and freshly ground black pepper. Bring to simmering point and cook, covered, for 20 minutes until rice is tender and liquid is absorbed. Stir in reserved prawns, scallops and cooked crayfish tails or crab pieces and cook, covered, for 5 minutes more until seafood is heated through. Garnish with fresh parsley and serve with boiled rice.

Serves 6.

——CHILLI-CHICKEN SALAD——

225 g (8 oz/1 ¼ cups) brown rice
3 tablespoons sesame oil
2 tablespoons peanut oil
150 g (5oz/1 cup) cashew nuts or peanuts
150 g (5 oz) mange tout (snow peas)
700 g (1 ½ lb) skinned and boned chicken breasts,
    cut into thin strips
2 tablespoons sunflower oil
2.5 cm (1 in) fresh ginger, peeled and thinly sliced
2 cloves garlic, finely chopped
4-6 spring onions, sliced
1-2 fresh green chillies, seeded and thinly sliced
3 tablespoons wine vinegar
2 tablespoons chopped fresh mint or coriander
mixed lettuce leaves
1 orange, peeled, segmented and any juice reserved

Cook rice for 30-35 minutes or according to directions, until tender. Drain and place in a large bowl; toss with sesame oil and set aside. Heat the wok until hot, add peanut oil and swirl to coat wok. Add the nuts and stir-fry for 1-2 minutes until they turn golden. Remove and add to rice. Add mange tout (snow peas) to oil in wok and stir-fry for 1-2 minutes until bright green. Add to the rice. Add chicken to the wok, in 2 batches, and stir-fry for 2-3 minutes until chicken turns white and feels firm to the touch. Add to the rice.

Add sunflower oil to wok and stir in ginger, garlic, spring onions and chillies. Stir-fry for 1 minute until onion begins to soften. Pour contents of wok over rice mixture. Return wok to heat and pour in vinegar, swirling to deglaze wok. Pour vinegar over rice mixture, add half the herbs and toss to mix well. Line a shallow serving bowl with lettuce. Spoon rice mixture on to leaves, decorate with orange segments and pour over any juice. Garnish with remaining herbs.

Serves 4.

LEMON CHICKEN

2 egg whites
7 teaspoons cornflour
575 g (1¼ lb) skinned and boned chicken breasts,
    cut into thin strips
115 ml (4 fl oz/½ cup) vegetable oil
1 onion, thinly sliced
1 clove garlic, finely chopped
1 red pepper (capsicum), thinly sliced
150 ml (5 fl oz/⅔ cup) chicken stock
grated rind and juice of 1 lemon
1 tablespoon sugar
1 tablespoon light soy sauce
1 tablespoon rice wine or dry sherry
dash hot pepper sauce
fresh chives, to garnish

In a medium bowl, beat egg whites with 4 teaspoons cornflour. Add the chicken strips and toss to coat well. Refrigerate for 10-15 minutes. In the wok, heat the vegetable oil until very hot and swirl to coat wok. Using tongs or a fork, add the chicken strips a few at a time. Stir-fry quickly to keep strips from sticking. Cook chicken strips for 2-3 minutes until just golden. Remove to absorbent kitchen paper to drain and pour off all but 1 tablespoon oil. (Reserve oil for future frying or discard.)

Add onion, garlic and red pepper (capsicum) to the wok. Stir-fry for 1-2 minutes until onion begins to soften. Add chicken stock, lemon rind and juice, sugar, soy sauce, wine or sherry and a few drops hot pepper sauce. Dissolve remaining cornflour in 2 table-spoons water and stir into the sauce. Cook for 30 seconds until sauce thickens. Add chicken strips and toss to coat. Cook for 1 minute, until chicken is heated through. Garnish with chives and serve with boiled rice.

Serves 4.

—— YELLOW BEAN CHICKEN ——

2 egg whites
4 teaspoons cornflour
700 g (1½ lb) skinned and boned chicken breasts or
    thighs, cut into 2.5 cm (1 in) cubes
115 ml (4 fl oz/½ cup) peanut oil
4 spring onions, sliced
2 stalks celery, thinly sliced
1 green pepper (capsicum), diced
1 teaspoon finely chopped fresh root ginger
1 teaspoon crushed chillies
1 teaspoon sugar
4 teaspoons yellow bean paste
4 teaspoons dry sherry or rice wine
150 g (5 oz/1 cup) cashew nuts, toasted
lemon wedges, to garnish

In a medium bowl, beat egg whites with the cornflour. Add chicken cubes, tossing to coat well. Refrigerate for 10-15 minutes. In the wok, heat peanut oil until very hot and swirl to coat wok. Using a slotted spoon, and working in 2 batches, lift out chicken cubes and add to wok. Stir-fry quickly to keep cubes from sticking. Cook chicken cubes for 2-3 minutes until just golden. Remove to absorbent kitchen paper to drain and pour off all but 2 tablespoons oil. (Reserve oil for future frying or discard.)

Add spring onions, celery, green pepper (capsicum) and ginger and stir-fry for 2-3 minutes until onion and pepper (capsicum) begin to soften. Stir in the crushed chillies, sugar, yellow bean paste, dry sherry or rice wine and the cashew nuts, tossing until sugar dissolves. Add chicken cubes and toss to coat; cook for 30 seconds. Serve immediately, garnished with lemon wedges and accompanied by a salad.

Serves 4.

—ARABIAN CHICKEN IN PITTA—

1 kg (2¼ lb) skinned and boned chicken breast,
   cut into thin slices
½ teaspoon freshly ground black pepper
½ teaspoon salt
½ teaspoon ground cardamon
½ teaspoon ground cinnamon
¼ teaspoon ground cloves
¼ teaspoon ground allspice
¼ teaspoon cayenne or chilli powder
2 tablespoons lemon juice
2 tablespoons olive oil
three 20 cm (8 in) pitta breads
6 lettuce leaves
1 onion, finely chopped
bottled tahini sauce
fresh basil sprigs and onion rings, to garnish

In a large shallow baking dish, combine chicken with black pepper, salt, ground cardamon, cinnamon, cloves, allspice, cayenne or chilli powder and lemon juice. Toss pieces of chicken in spice mixture to coat well and leave to marinate in the refrigerator for 4-6 hours or overnight. Heat the wok until hot. Add the olive oil and swirl to coat wok. Add coated chicken pieces and, working in 2 batches, stir-fry for 2-3 minutes until just golden and firm to the touch. Remove chicken to absorbent kitchen paper to drain.

Preheat grill. Arrange pittas on a grill rack and heat under grill for 1-2 minutes, turning once during cooking, until pittas are puffed and golden. Cut each pitta crosswise in half to open, and place a lettuce leaf in each half. Spoon equal amounts of chicken strips into pittas, sprinkle with chopped onion and drizzle with tahini sauce. Garnish with basil sprigs and onion rings.

Serves 6.

CHICKEN IN BALSAMIC VINEGAR

mixed salad leaves for serving
2 tablespoons olive oil
1 onion, finely chopped
2 cloves garlic, finely minced or crushed
700 g (1½ lb) skinned and boned chicken breasts, cut
    into 2.5 cm (1 in) strips
9 teaspoons balsamic vinegar
3 teaspoons Dijon mustard
freshly ground black pepper
2 tablespoons shredded fresh basil
fresh basil leaves, to garnish

Arrange salad leaves on 4 dinner plates and
set aside.

Heat the wok until hot. Add olive oil and
swirl to coat wok. Add onion and garlic and
stir-fry for 1-2 minutes until onion begins to
soften. Add chicken strips, working in 2
batches, and stir-fry for 3-4 minutes until
golden and chicken feels firm to the touch.
Return all chicken to the wok.

Stir in vinegar and mustard and stir-fry for
2-3 minutes until chicken is cooked through
and well coated with vinegar and mustard.
Season with pepper and sprinkle with shredded basil. Spoon onto salad-lined plates and
garnish with additional basil leaves. Serve
with sautéed potatoes.

Serves 4.

SATAY-STYLE CHICKEN

lettuce leaves and cucumber sticks for serving
3 tablespoons peanut oil
2.5 cm (1 in) piece fresh root ginger, peeled and
    finely chopped
1 clove garlic, finely chopped
575 g (1¼ lb) skinned and boned chicken thighs,
    cut into small pieces
1 teaspoon chilli powder
2 tablespoons crunchy or smooth peanut butter
6 teaspoons Chinese chilli sauce
4-6 spring onions, thinly sliced
300 ml (10 fl oz/1¼ cups) unsweetened coconut milk
1 teaspoon sugar
½ teaspoon salt
chopped peanuts and fresh coriander leaves, to garnish

Arrange lettuce leaves and cucumber sticks on a shallow serving dish and set aside. Heat the wok until hot. Add oil and swirl to coat wok. Add ginger and garlic and stir-fry for 1 minute, until fragrant; do not brown. Add chicken and stir-fry for 3-4 minutes until just golden and pieces feel slightly firm to the touch.

Stir in chilli powder, peanut butter, chilli sauce and the spring onions. Slowly add coconut milk, stirring until sauce is smooth. Add sugar and salt and simmer for 3-5 minutes until sauce is thickened. Spoon onto a serving dish and sprinkle with chopped peanuts and coriander leaves. Serve with rice.

Serves 4.

—— BANG BANG CHICKEN ——

55 ml (2 fl oz/¼ cup) peanut oil
3 carrots, cut into julienne strips
1 fresh chilli, seeded and chopped
225 g (8 oz) beansprouts, trimmed
½ cucumber, seeded and cut into julienne strips
800 g (1¾ lb) skinned and boned chicken breasts,
    cut into shreds
2.5 cm (1 in) fresh ginger, cut in julienne strips
2 cloves garlic, finely chopped
4 spring onions, thinly sliced
9 teaspoons cider vinegar or rice vinegar
2 tablespoons dry sherry or rice wine
1 tablespoon sugar
1 teaspoon Chinese chilli sauce
150 ml (5 fl oz/⅔ cup) chicken stock
3 tablespoons each light soy sauce and tahini

Heat wok until hot. Add 2 tablespoons peanut oil and swirl to coat wok. Add carrots and
chilli and stir-fry for 2-3 minutes. Remove to
a bowl. Stir-fry beansprouts for 1 minute and
remove to bowl. Add cucumber to bowl.
Heat remaining oil in wok and add chicken.
Working in 2 batches, stir-fry for 2-3 minutes
until the chicken is white and the juices run
clear. Remove to another bowl. Increase
heat, add ginger and garlic to wok and stir-fry
for 1 minute. Add spring onions and stir-fry
for 1 minute. Add remaining ingredients and
stir-fry until sauce is smooth and thick.

Pour half the sauce over carrot mixture and
remaining sauce over chicken; toss each mixture well. Spoon chicken onto centre of a
serving dish, then spoon vegetables around
chicken. Serve with rice or noodles.

Serves 6.

Note: Garnish with sesame seeds or chopped
peanuts and coriander, if wished.

— MOROCCAN-STYLE CHICKEN —

1.35 kg (3 lb) chicken, cut into 8 pieces
4 tablespoons olive oil
grated rind and juice of 1 lemon
1 teaspoon each ground cinnamon, ground ginger and
    ground cumin
½ teaspoon salt
½ teaspoon cayenne pepper (or to taste)
1 onion, chopped
3-4 cloves garlic, finely chopped
1 red pepper (capsicum), diced
1 tomato, peeled, seeded and chopped
250 ml (9 fl oz/1 cup) chicken stock or water
16 stoned prunes
55 ml (2 fl oz/¼ cup) honey
1 large lemon, thinly sliced
toasted almonds and chopped fresh parsley, to garnish

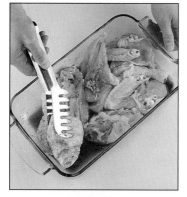

In a large shallow baking dish, combine chicken pieces with 2 tablespoons olive oil, the lemon rind and juice, cinnamon, ginger, cumin, salt and cayenne pepper to taste. Work the spices into the chicken pieces, cover and leave to marinate in the refrigerator for 4-6 hours or overnight. Heat the wok until hot. Add 1 tablespoon oil and swirl to coat. Arrange marinated chicken pieces on bottom and side of wok in a single layer and stir-fry for 6-8 minutes, until golden brown. Remove chicken pieces to the cleaned baking dish.

Add remaining oil, onion, garlic and red pepper (capsicum) to wok. Stir-fry for 2-3 minutes. Add tomato and stock or water and bring to simmering point, stirring. Return chicken and marinade to sauce. Simmer, covered, for 35-40 minutes until chicken is tender, adding prunes, honey and lemon slices after 20 minutes cooking. Remove chicken to serving dish, spoon sauce over and sprinkle with almonds and parsley. Serve with couscous.

Serves 4.

SPICY CHICKEN WINGS

1 tablespoon light soy sauce
1 tablespoon dry sherry or rice wine
1 kg (2 ¼ lb) chicken wings, tips removed and wings
   cut into 2 pieces at joint
1 tablespoon peanut oil
2.5 cm (1 in) fresh ginger, peeled and finely chopped
2 cloves garlic, finely chopped
3 tablespoons black beans, coarsely chopped
115 ml (4 fl oz/½ cup) chicken stock
2 tablespoons soy sauce
1 teaspoon Chinese chilli sauce
4-6 spring onions, thinly sliced
175 g (6 oz) thin green beans, cut into 5 cm
   (2 in) pieces
2 tablespoons chopped peanuts and fresh coriander
   leaves, to garnish

In a shallow baking dish, combine soy sauce, dry sherry or rice wine and chicken wings. Toss well and leave to stand, covered, 1 hour. Heat the wok until hot. Add peanut oil and swirl to coat wok. Add ginger and garlic and stir-fry for 1 minute. Working in 2 batches if necessary, add chicken wings and stir-fry for 3-5 minutes until golden brown. Stir in black beans, stock, soy sauce and chilli sauce. If working in batches, return all chicken wings to the wok.

Bring to the boil, reduce the heat and cook for 4-6 minutes, stirring frequently. Stir in spring onions and green beans and cook for 2-3 minutes more until chicken is tender and juices run clear. Sprinkle with chopped peanuts and garnish with coriander leaves.

Serves 4-6.

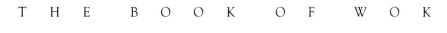

— TANGERINE CHICKEN WINGS —

1 onion, thinly sliced
2.5 cm (1 in) piece fresh root ginger, peeled and
  thinly sliced
1 teaspoon sea salt
4 tablespoons dry sherry or rice wine
4 tablespoons soy sauce
16 chicken wings, wing tips removed
1 large tangerine
70 ml (2½ fl oz/⅓ cup) vegetable oil
2 fresh chillies, seeded and chopped
4 spring onions, thinly sliced
2 teaspoons sugar
3 teaspoons wine vinegar
1 teaspoon sesame oil
fresh coriander sprigs, to garnish

In a large shallow baking dish, combine
onion, ginger, salt, 1 tablespoon sherry or
rice wine and 1 tablespoon soy sauce. Add
chicken wings and toss to coat well. Leave
to stand 30 minutes. Remove rind from
tangerine and slice thinly. Squeeze 2-3 tablespoons tangerine juice and reserve. Heat oil
in wok until hot and swirl to coat wok.
Remove chicken from the marinade, return-
ing any onion or ginger sticking to it. Working in 2 batches, add chicken wings to wok.
Fry for 3-4 minutes until golden, turning
once. Drain on absorbent kitchen paper.

Pour off all but 1 tablespoon oil from wok.
Add chillies, spring onions and tangerine
rind and stir-fry for 30-40 seconds. Pour in
reserved marinade with the onion and ginger
slices. Add sugar, vinegar and remaining
sherry or rice wine, soy sauce and tangerine
juice. Add the chicken wings and toss to coat
well; cook for 1 minute until heated through.
Drizzle with sesame oil and garnish with
coriander sprigs. Serve with noodles tossed in
sesame oil and sesame seeds, if wished.

Serves 4.

— BOMBAY CHICKEN THIGHS —

2 tablespoons vegetable oil
2.5 cm (1 in) piece fresh root ginger, peeled and
 finely chopped
2 cloves garlic, finely chopped
1 fresh chilli, seeded and chopped
700 g (1 ½ lb) skinned and boned chicken thighs,
 cut into pieces
1 onion, coarsely chopped
2 teaspoons curry paste
400 g (14 oz) can chopped tomatoes
1 teaspoon ground coriander
grated rind and juice of ½ lemon
2 bay leaves
freshly ground black pepper
150 ml (5 fl oz/⅔ cup) unsweetened coconut milk
fresh coriander or lemon leaves, to garnish

Heat the wok until hot. Add oil and swirl to
coat wok. Add ginger, garlic and chilli and
stir-fry for 1 minute until very fragrant. Add
chicken pieces and stir-fry for 3-4 minutes
until chicken begins to colour. Stir in onion
and curry paste and stir to coat. Add tomatoes and their juice, coriander, lemon rind
and juice, bay leaves and black pepper. Bring
to simmering point and cook for 3-4 minutes
until sauce is slightly thickened.

Stir in coconut milk and reduce heat. Simmer for 5-6 minutes until sauce is thickened
and chicken pieces are tender. Remove bay
leaves and garnish with coriander or lemon
leaves. Serve with steamed basmati rice.

Serves 4.

— SZECHUAN CHICKEN LIVERS —

25 g (1 oz) dried Chinese mushrooms or 115 g (4 oz)
    mushrooms, quartered
1 teaspoon Szechuan peppercorns
2 tablespoons vegetable oil
450 g (1 lb) chicken livers, trimmed and cut in half
2.5 cm (1 in) piece fresh root ginger, peeled and
    finely chopped
2 cloves garlic, finely chopped
4-6 spring onions, thinly sliced
2 teaspoons cornflour, dissolved in 2 tablespoons water
2 tablespoons soy sauce
2 tablespoons rice wine or dry sherry
½ teaspoon sugar
spring onions, to garnish

If using dried mushrooms, place in a bowl, cover with warm water and soak for 20-25 minutes. Using a slotted spoon, carefully remove mushrooms from water, to avoid disturbing any grit which has sunk to the bottom. Reserve liquid. Squeeze mushrooms dry, then cut off and discard stems. Heat wok until hot. Add Szechuan peppercorns and dry-fry for 2-3 minutes until very fragrant. Pour into bowl to cool. When cold, crush in a mortar and pestle or grind in a spice grinder. Set aside.

Heat wok until hot. Add oil and swirl to coat. Pat livers dry and stir-fry for 2-3 minutes. Add ginger, garlic, mushrooms and spring onions. Stir-fry for 2 minutes, until livers are brown. Add 2 tablespoons mushroom liquid if using dried mushrooms or 2 tablespoons water if using fresh mushrooms, to dissolved cornflour. Stir into wok with soy sauce, wine or sherry, peppercorns and sugar. Stir until thickened. Garnish with spring onions and serve with rice.

Serves 4.

—JAPANESE CHICKEN LIVERS—

2 tablespoons light soy sauce
2 tablespoons mirin or dry sherry mixed with
  ½ teaspoon sugar
450 g (1 lb) chicken livers, trimmed and cut in half
2 tablespoons vegetable oil
1 green pepper (capsicum), diced
4 spring onions, sliced
1 clove garlic, finely chopped
2.5 cm (1 in) piece fresh root ginger, peeled and
  finely chopped
¼ teaspoon cayenne pepper
2 tablespoons sugar
3 tablespoons dark soy sauce
1 teaspoon sesame oil
julienne strips of radish, to garnish (optional)

In a shallow dish, combine the light soy sauce, mirin or sweetened sherry and chicken livers. Leave to marinate for 20-30 minutes, stirring occasionally. Heat the wok until hot. Add oil and swirl to coat wok. With a slotted spoon, remove chicken livers from the marinade and add to wok. Stir-fry for 3-4 minutes, until beginning to brown. Add green pepper (capsicum), spring onions, garlic and ginger and stir-fry for a further 1-2 minutes. The chicken livers should be browned, but still pink inside.

Stir in cayenne pepper, sugar and dark soy sauce and toss to coat well. Drizzle with the sesame oil and serve immediately, garnished with radish, if wished.

Serves 4.

—— DUCK WITH SPINACH ——

4 slices bacon, diced
700 g (1½ lb) duckling breast fillet, skinned and excess
    fat removed, cut crosswise into thin strips
225 g (8 oz) wild or field mushrooms, sliced
1 clove garlic, finely chopped
1 onion, thinly sliced
2 tablespoons lemon juice
salt and freshly ground black pepper
5 tablespoons olive oil
450 g (1 lb) fresh baby spinach leaves
6 teaspoons red wine vinegar
1 teaspoon Dijon mustard
2 tablespoons pine nuts, toasted, to garnish

Place bacon in the cold wok. Heat the wok over moderate heat until bacon begins to release its fat. Stir-fry for 2-3 minutes until crisp. With a slotted spoon, remove to a bowl. Increase heat. Add duckling strips to bacon fat in wok, working in 2 batches if necessary, and stir-fry for 3-5 minutes until brown and crisp. Remove to same bowl. Pour off all but 1 tablespoon fat from wok and add mushrooms, garlic, onion and lemon juice. Stir-fry for 2-3 minutes until liquid has evaporated. Remove to bowl, season and mix well. Wipe wok dry.

Add 1 tablespoon olive oil to wok and swirl to coat wok. Add spinach and stir-fry for 1 minute until spinach just wilts and turns bright green. Divide among 4 dinner plates. Pour remaining oil into wok, add the vinegar and mustard and stir to blend. Pour the liquid over the duckling mixture in bowl and toss well to mix. Spoon equal amounts of duckling mixture over the spinach on each plate and sprinkle with toasted pine nuts. Serve with sautéed potatoes, if wished.

Serves 4.

——— DUCK IN GINGER SAUCE ———

3 tablespoons olive oil
1 onion, chopped, and 5-6 cloves garlic, chopped
5 cm (2 in) piece of fresh root ginger, peeled and sliced
1 tablespoon plain flour
115 ml (4 fl oz/½ cup) red wine
250 ml (9 fl oz/1 cup) port
3-4 sprigs each fresh thyme and rosemary
2 bay leaves
1 tablespoon black peppercorns
685 ml (24 fl oz/3 cups) veal, duck or chicken stock
700 g (1½ lb) duckling breast fillet, skinned and excess
    fat removed, cut crosswise into thin strips
450 g (1 lb) shiitake mushrooms, sliced
75 g (3 oz) raisins
6 spring onions, cut into 5 cm (2 in) pieces
450 g (1 lb) pappardelle or wide egg noodles

Heat wok until hot. Add 2 tablespoons of the
oil and swirl to coat wok. Add onion, garlic
and ginger and stir-fry for 2-3 minutes until
onion is softened. Stir in flour until completely blended. Slowly pour in wine, stirring
until thickened and blended. Add port,
thyme, rosemary, bay leaves, peppercorns
and stock. Bring to the boil and skim any
foam which comes to the surface. Simmer,
stirring often, for 15-20 minutes until lightly
thickened and reduced by about half. Strain
into a bowl.

Wipe wok and heat until very hot, but not
smoking. Add remaining oil and swirl to coat
wok. Add duckling strips and cook for 2-3
minutes until golden. Remove to a bowl. Stir
in mushrooms, raisins and spring onions and
stir-fry for 2-3 minutes. Add sauce and bring
to simmering point. Add duckling strips.
Cook pappardelle or egg noodles according
to packet directions. Drain and place in a
serving dish. Toss with a little of the sauce,
then pour over the remaining sauce.

Serves 4.

—DUCK WITH BEETS & BEANS—

1 tablespoon olive oil
2 large duckling breast fillets, 250 g (8 oz) each, boned
　　with fat removed and skin left on
4 shallots, finely chopped
1 clove garlic, finely sliced
350 g (12 oz) wild or field mushrooms, trimmed
1 tablespoon plain flour
2 tablespoons fruity red wine
150 ml (5 fl oz/²⁄₃ cup) duck or chicken stock
225 g (8 oz) fresh or frozen broad (lima) beans
1 tablespoon redcurrant jelly
freshly ground black pepper
1 teaspoon cornflour
½ teaspoon dry mustard powder
grated rind and juice of 1 large orange
450 g (1 lb) fresh baby beets, cooked and peeled

Heat wok until hot. Add oil and swirl to coat.
With a sharp knife, remove skin and make
2 or 3 diagonal slashes across duckling
breasts, 1 cm (½ in) deep. Add to wok and
cook over moderate heat for 5-6 minutes
until golden, turning and stirring. Remove to
a plate and keep warm. Add shallots and
garlic to wok. Stir-fry for 1 minute, then
add mushrooms and stir-fry for 2-3 minutes.
Sprinkle over flour and stir to blend. Add
wine and stock and bring to the boil.
Add beans.

Simmer, covered, for 15-20 minutes until
beans are tender and sauce is thickened.
(If using frozen beans, add 5 minutes before
end of cooking time.) Stir in redcurrant jelly
and season with pepper. Meanwhile, in a
saucepan, combine cornflour, mustard
powder, rind and juice of the orange and
beets. Bring to the boil and simmer for
1 minute until glaze thickens and beets are
hot. Slice duck thinly; arrange slices on
4 plates with beans and beets.

Serves 4.

DUCK WITH PLUMS

2 tablespoons vegetable oil
700 g (1½ lb) duckling breast fillets, skinned and
    excess fat removed, cut crosswise into thin strips
225 g (8 oz) red plums, stoned and thinly sliced
55 ml (2 fl oz/¼ cup) port
6 teaspoons wine vinegar
grated rind and juice of 1 orange
2 tablespoons Chinese plum or duck sauce
4 spring onions, cut into thin strips
1 tablespoon soy sauce
3-4 whole cloves
small piece cinnamon stick
½ teaspoon Chinese chilli sauce (or to taste)
fresh parsley and grated orange rind, to garnish

Heat the wok until hot. Add oil and swirl to coat wok. Add duckling breast strips and stir-fry for 3-4 minutes until golden. Remove to a bowl. Add plums, port, wine vinegar, rind and juice of the orange, plum or duck sauce, spring onions, soy sauce, cloves, cinnamon stick and chilli sauce to taste. Bring to simmering point and cook gently for 4-5 minutes until plums begin to soften.

Return duckling strips to wok and stir-fry for 2 minutes until duck is heated through and sauce is thickened. Garnish with parsley and grated orange rind. Serve with noodles or rice tossed with sesame seeds.

Serves 4.

TURKEY CHILLI

700 g (1½ lb) small turkey thighs
2-3 tablespoons vegetable oil
1 onion, chopped
4 cloves garlic, finely chopped
1-2 fresh chillies, seeded and chopped
4 teaspoons chilli powder
cayenne pepper, to taste
1½ teaspoons ground cumin
400 g (14 oz) can peeled tomatoes
1½ teaspoons soft brown sugar
salt
two 425 g (15 oz) cans red kidney beans
sour cream and chopped fresh parsley, to garnish

With a small, sharp knife, remove skin from turkey and discard. Slice meat from thigh bones; cut into small pieces. Heat the wok until hot. Add 1 tablespoon oil and swirl to coat wok. Add half the turkey meat and stir-fry for 4-5 minutes until brown. Remove to a bowl; repeat with remaining turkey meat, adding a little more oil if necessary. Remove meat to bowl. Add remaining oil to wok and add onion and garlic. Stir-fry for 3-4 minutes, until onion softens. Stir in chillies, chilli powder, cayenne pepper and ground cumin.

Stir in tomatoes, with their liquid, then add the sugar and season with salt. Add turkey and kidney beans to the wok. Bring mixture to the boil and reduce heat. Simmer, covered, for 45-55 minutes. Remove cover and cook 15 minutes more until chilli is thick and well reduced. Taste and adjust seasoning, if necessary. Garnish with sour cream and chopped parsley and serve with rice.

Serves 6-8.

—GREEN PEPPERCORN TURKEY—

2 tablespoons olive oil
700 g (1½ lb) boneless turkey breast fillets
1 clove garlic, finely chopped
4 spring onions, thinly sliced
1 tablespoon green peppercorns
55 ml (2 fl oz/¼ cup) brandy or white wine
115 ml (4 fl oz/½ cup) whipping cream
½ teaspoon salt
1 pear or apple, cut in half lengthwise, cored and cut
    lengthwise into thin slices
toasted slivered almonds and fresh chives, to garnish

Heat the wok until hot. Add oil and swirl to coat wok. Arrange turkey in wok in a single layer, working in 2 batches, if necessary.

Cook for 3-5 minutes, turning halfway through cooking. Remove to serving plate and keep warm. Add garlic, spring onions and green peppercorns to wok and stir-fry for 1 minute until onions begin to soften. Add brandy or wine and stir to deglaze. Cook for 1-2 minutes to reduce slightly.

Stir in whipping cream and salt and bring to the boil. Reduce heat and add pear or apple slices. Cook, covered, for 1-2 minutes until fruit slices are heated through, then arrange them over turkey breast fillets. Pour sauce over and sprinkle with toasted almonds and chives. Serve with mange tout (snow peas).

Serves 4.

TURKEY MARSALA

70 ml (2½ fl oz/⅓ cup) sweet Marsala
3 tablespoons raisins
25 g (1 oz/2 tablespoons) butter
4 leeks (pale green and white parts only), cut in half
    lengthwise and sliced
250 ml (9 fl oz/1 cup) chicken stock
1 bay leaf
½ teaspoon dried thyme
¼ teaspoon dried rubbed sage
575 g (1¼ lb) boneless turkey breast fillets, cut into
    strips
finely grated rind of 1 lemon
2 teaspoons plain flour
2 tablespoons whipping cream
fresh sage leaves and lemon slices, to garnish

In a small bowl, combine Marsala with the raisins. Leave to stand 20 minutes. Heat the wok until hot. Add 1 tablespoon butter and swirl to melt and coat wok. Add leeks and stir-fry for 1 minute. Add 70 ml (2½ fl oz/ ⅓ cup) chicken stock, bay leaf, thyme and sage and cook, covered, for 4-6 minutes until leeks are tender and liquid has evaporated. Discard bay leaf. Remove to a bowl and cover to keep warm. Wipe wok dry.

Add remaining butter to wok and swirl to coat. Add the turkey, in 2 batches, and stir-fry for 2 minutes. Remove to a plate. Cook lemon rind and flour for 1 minute. Slowly add remaining stock and bring to the boil. Add Marsala, raisins and cream and simmer for 2 minutes. Spoon leek mixture onto plates, top with turkey and spoon sauce over. Garnish with sage and lemon. Serve with rice.

Serves 4.

— TURKEY WITH CHILLI RELISH —

700 g (1½ lb) boneless turkey breast fillets,
  cut into strips
3-4 tablespoons seasoned flour
3-4 tablespoons vegetable oil
70 ml (2½ fl oz/⅓ cup) chicken stock
2 tablespoons cider vinegar
½ teaspoon chilli powder
cayenne pepper, to taste
2-3 plum tomatoes, peeled, seeded and chopped
1 red onion, finely chopped
1 fresh chilli, seeded and chopped
1 dessert apple, cored and chopped
2 tablespoons chopped fresh coriander
1 tablespoon chopped peanuts or walnuts

Dredge the turkey strips in the seasoned flour.

Heat the wok until hot. Add 2 tablespoons oil and swirl to coat wok. Add half the turkey strips and stir-fry for 1-2 minutes. Remove to serving plate; keep warm. Add 1-2 tablespoons more oil and cook remaining strips in the same way. Remove to the serving plate and keep warm.

Add stock and stir to deglaze the wok. Add cider vinegar, chilli powder, cayenne pepper to taste, tomatoes, onion, chilli and chopped apple. Cook for 1-2 minutes until sauce thickens. Return turkey strips to wok and stir them into the sauce. Sprinkle with coriander and peanuts or walnuts. Serve with pasta.

Serves 4.

CREAMY PAPRIKA TURKEY

55 g (2 oz/4 tablespoons) butter
1 onion, finely chopped
1 teaspoon paprika
250 ml (9 fl oz/1 cup) whipping cream
3 teaspoons Dijon mustard
2 tablespoons chopped fresh dill
salt and freshly ground black pepper
700 g (1½ lb) turkey breast fillets, cut crosswise into
    2.5 cm (1 in) strips
6 tablespoons seasoned flour
2 tablespoons vegetable oil
225 g (8 oz) tagliatelle or egg noodles
300 g (10 oz) frozen peas
2 teaspoons caraway seeds
fresh dill sprigs, to garnish

Heat wok until hot. Add 1 tablespoon butter and swirl to coat wok. Add onion and stir-fry for 7-8 minutes. Add paprika and cook for 1 minute. Add cream and bring to simmering point; cook for 1-2 minutes until slightly thickened. Add mustard and dill and season. Pour into small bowl; keep warm. Wipe wok clean. Dredge turkey strips in seasoned flour. Heat the wok until hot. Add vegetable oil and 1 tablespoon butter and swirl to coat wok. Add turkey strips, working in batches, and stir-fry for 2-3 minutes. Remove to plate and keep warm.

Cook tagliatelle according to packet directions; drain well. Heat the wok until hot. Add remaining butter, peas and caraway seeds. Stir-fry for for 2-3 minutes until peas are tender. Stir in noodles and season. Stir in a spoonful of the reserved sauce and toss to coat noodles. Turn out onto serving plate. Pour remaining sauce and turkey strips into the wok, tossing to coat. Cook for 1 minute. Spoon turkey strips and sauce over noodles. Garnish with dill sprigs.

Serves 4.

── TURKEY WITH BROCCOLI ──

1 tablespoon vegetable oil
450 g (1 lb) boneless turkey cutlets, cut into thin strips
1 tablespoon sesame oil
450 g (1 lb) broccoli, stems and florets cut into 2.5 cm
  (1 in) pieces
4 spring onions, cut into 2.5 cm (1 in) pieces
2.5 cm (1 in) piece of fresh root ginger, peeled and cut
  into julienne strips
2 cloves garlic, finely chopped
55 ml (2 fl oz/¼ cup) dry sherry or rice wine
2 tablespoons light soy sauce
2 teaspoons cornflour dissolved in 1 tablespoon water
55 ml (2 fl oz/¼ cup) chicken stock
225 g (8 oz) canned water chestnuts, rinsed and sliced
fresh coriander, to garnish

Heat the wok until very hot but not smoking. Add vegetable oil and swirl to coat wok. Add turkey strips and stir-fry for 2-3 minutes until beginning to colour. Remove to a bowl. Add sesame oil to wok. Add broccoli and stir-fry for 2 minutes. Add the spring onions, ginger, and garlic and stir-fry for 2-3 minutes more, until broccoli is tender but still crisp.

Add dry sherry or rice wine and soy sauce and cook for 2 minutes. Stir dissolved cornflour and stir into chicken stock; stir into wok. Stir-fry for 1 minute until sauce bubbles and thickens. Add reserved turkey strips and water chestnuts, tossing to coat, and cook for 1 minute until turkey is heated through. Garnish with coriander and serve with rice and wild rice.

Serves 4.

—TURKEY WITH APRICOTS—

2 tablespoons olive oil
700 g (1½ lb) boneless turkey breast fillets
½ teaspoon dried thyme
salt and freshly ground black pepper
4 shallots, thinly sliced
25 g (1 oz/3 tablespoons) cranberries
45 g (1½ oz/¼ cup) dried apricots, chopped
1 small green pepper (capsicum), diced
2 tablespoons cider vinegar
55 ml (2 fl oz/¼ cup) dry white wine or apple juice
115 ml (4 fl oz/½ cup) chicken stock
1-2 tablespoons apricot preserve
1 tablespoon honey
chopped fresh parsley or thyme, to garnish

Heat wok until hot. Add oil and swirl to coat wok. Arrange turkey breast fillets on bottom and up side of wok in single layer, working in 2 batches, if necessary. Sprinkle with the thyme and season with salt and pepper. Cook fillets for 2-3 minutes, turning them halfway through cooking. Remove to serving plate; keep warm.

Add shallots, cranberries, apricots and green pepper (capsicum) and stir-fry for 1 minute. Stir in cider vinegar, white wine or apple juice, chicken stock, apricot preserve and honey. Bring to the boil and simmer for 3-4 minutes until sauce thickens slightly and fruit is tender. Spoon sauce and fruits over turkey fillets and garnish with parsley or thyme. Serve with wild rice.

Serves 4.

SPICY SESAME BEEF

1 tablespoon cornflour
3 tablespoons light soy sauce
450 g (1 lb) rump, sirloin or fillet steak, cut crosswise
　　into thin strips
350 g (12 oz) broccoli
2 tablespoons sesame oil
2.5 cm (1 in) piece fresh root ginger, peeled and cut into
　　julienne strips
2 cloves garlic, finely chopped
1 fresh chilli, seeded and thinly sliced
1 red pepper (capsicum), thinly sliced
400 g (14 oz) baby corn
115 ml (4 fl oz/½ cup) beef or chicken stock, or water
4-6 spring onions, cut into 5 cm (2 in) pieces
toasted sesame seeds, to garnish

In a bowl, combine cornflour and soy sauce. Add beef strips and toss to coat well. Leave to stand for 20 minutes. Cut large flowerets from the broccoli and divide into small flowerets. With a swivel-bladed vegetable peeler, peel the stalk and cut diagonally into 2.5 cm (1 in) pieces. Heat the wok until very hot. Add sesame oil and swirl to coat. Add beef strips and marinade and stir-fry for 2-3 minutes until browned.

With a slotted spoon, remove beef strips to a bowl. Add ginger, garlic and chilli to the wok and stir-fry for 1 minute. Add broccoli, red pepper (capsicum) and baby corn and stir-fry for 2-3 minutes until broccoli is tender but still crisp. Add the stock and stir for 1 minute until sauce bubbles and thickens. Add spring onions and reserved beef strips and stir-fry for 1-2 minutes until beef strips are heated through. Sprinkle with sesame seeds and serve with rice or noodles.

Serves 4.

TERIYAKI STEAKS

55 ml (2 fl oz/¼ cup) mirin or dry sherry sweetened
  with 1 teaspoon sugar
55 ml (2 fl oz/¼ cup) light soy sauce
1 cm (½ in) piece fresh root ginger, peeled and minced
1 clove garlic, finely chopped
1 teaspoon sugar
½ teaspoon red pepper sauce (or to taste)
4 sirloin or fillet steaks, cut into strips
2 tablespoons sesame oil
4 spring onions, thinly sliced
fresh coriander leaves, to garnish

In a shallow baking dish, combine mirin or
sweetened dry sherry, soy sauce, ginger,
garlic, sugar and red pepper sauce to taste.

Add the steak strips and turn to coat well.
Leave to stand for 1 hour, turning strips once
or twice.

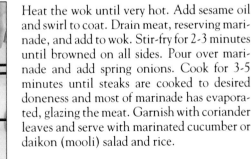

Heat the wok until very hot. Add sesame oil
and swirl to coat. Drain meat, reserving marinade, and add to wok. Stir-fry for 2-3 minutes
until browned on all sides. Pour over marinade and add spring onions. Cook for 3-5
minutes until steaks are cooked to desired
doneness and most of marinade has evaporated, glazing the meat. Garnish with coriander
leaves and serve with marinated cucumber or
daikon (mooli) salad and rice.

Serves 4.

—CHILLI BEEF WITH PEPPERS—

1 tablespoon cornflour
55 ml (2 fl oz/¼ cup) light soy sauce
1 tablespoon honey or brown sugar
1 teaspoon Chinese chilli sauce
2 tablespoons vegetable oil
450 g (1 lb) rump or sirloin steak, cut crosswise into
   thin strips
1 tablespoon sesame oil
2 cloves garlic, finely chopped
1 chilli, seeded and thinly sliced
1 onion, thinly sliced
1 red pepper (capsicum), cut into thin strips
1 green pepper (capsicum), cut into thin strips
1 yellow pepper (capsicum), cut into thin strips

In a small bowl, dissolve the cornflour with 55 ml (2 fl oz/¼ cup) water. Stir in the soy sauce, honey or sugar and chilli sauce until blended. Set aside. Heat the wok until very hot. Add vegetable oil and swirl to coat wok. Add beef strips and stir-fry for 2-3 minutes until beef is browned. With a slotted spoon, remove beef to a bowl.

Add sesame oil to the wok and add garlic and chilli. Stir-fry for 1 minute until fragrant. Add onion and pepper (capsicum) strips and stir-fry for 2-3 minutes until beginning to soften. Stir cornflour mixture, then stir into wok and stir until sauce bubbles and begins to thicken. Add beef strips and any juices and stir-fry for 1 minute until beef is heated through. Serve with rice.

Serves 4.

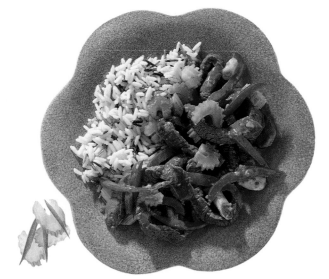

BEEF IN OYSTER SAUCE

3 teaspoons cornflour
1½ tablespoons soy sauce
1½ tablespoons rice wine or dry sherry
450 g (1 lb) rump, sirloin or fillet steak, cut crosswise
    into thin strips
2 tablespoons sesame oil
1 cm (½ in) piece fresh root ginger, peeled and chopped
2 cloves garlic, finely chopped
4 stalks celery, sliced
1 red pepper (capsicum), sliced
115 g (4 oz) mushrooms, sliced
4 spring onions, sliced
2 tablespoons oyster sauce
115 ml (4 fl oz/½ cup) chicken stock or water

In a bowl, combine 2 teaspoons of the cornflour with soy sauce and rice wine or sherry.
Add beef strips and toss to coat well. Allow to
stand for 25 minutes. Heat the wok until very
hot. Add oil and swirl to coat wok. Add beef
strips and stir-fry for 2-3 minutes until
browned. With a slotted spoon, remove to a
bowl. Add ginger and garlic to oil remaining
in wok and stir-fry for 1 minute. Add the
celery, red pepper (capsicum), mushrooms
and spring onions and stir-fry for 2-3 minutes
until vegetables begin to soften.

Stir in oyster sauce and combine remaining
cornflour with the stock or water, then stir
into the wok and bring to the boil. Add
reserved beef strips and toss beef and vegetables for 1 minute until sauce bubbles and
thickens and beef is heated through. Serve
with rice and wild rice.

Serves 4.

DRY-FRIED BEEF STRIPS

2 tablespoons sesame oil
450 g (1 lb) rump or sirloin steak, cut crosswise
   into julienne strips
2 tablespoons rice wine or dry sherry
1 tablespoon light soy sauce
2 cloves garlic, finely chopped
1 cm (½ in) piece fresh root ginger, peeled and
   finely chopped
1 tablespoon Chinese chilli bean paste (sauce)
2 teaspoons sugar
1 carrot, peeled and cut into julienne strips
2 stalks celery, cut into julienne strips
2-3 spring onions, thinly sliced
¼ teaspoon ground Szechuan pepper
cucumber matchsticks, to garnish

Heat the wok until very hot. Add the oil and swirl to coat wok. Add beef and stir-fry for 15 seconds to quickly seal meat. Add 1 tablespoon rice wine or sherry and stir-fry for 1-2 minutes until beef is browned. Pour off and reserve any excess liquid and continue stir-frying until beef is dry.

Stir in soy sauce, garlic, ginger, chilli bean paste, sugar, remaining rice wine or sherry and any reserved cooking juices and stir to blend well. Add carrot, celery, spring onions and ground Szechuan pepper and stir-fry until the vegetables begin to soften and all the liquid is absorbed. Garnish with cucumber matchsticks and serve with rice and wild rice.

Serves 4.

— THAI BEEF WITH NOODLES —

55 ml (2 fl oz/¼ cup) rice wine or dry sherry
2 tablespoons light soy sauce
2 cloves garlic, finely chopped
2.5 cm (1 in) piece fresh root ginger, peeled and
    finely chopped
½ teaspoon dried crushed chillies
450 g (1 lb) sirloin or fillet steak, 2.5 cm (1 in) thick,
    cut crosswise into 1 cm (½ in) strips
350 g (12 oz) ramen noodles or thin spaghetti
1 tablespoon sesame oil
115 g (4 oz) mange tout (snow peas)
4-6 spring onions, cut into 5 cm (2 in) pieces
2 teaspoons cornflour dissolved in 55 ml
    (2 fl oz/¼ cup) water
2 tablespoons chopped fresh coriander
fresh coriander leaves and lime slices, to garnish

In a shallow baking dish, combine wine or
sherry, soy sauce, garlic, ginger and chillies.
Add steak, cover and leave to marinate for
30 minutes, turning once. Cook noodles or
spaghetti according to packet directions,
rinse, drain and set aside. Heat wok until very
hot. Add sesame oil and swirl to coat wok.
Remove steak from marinade, scraping off
any ginger and garlic and reserving marinade.
Pat steak dry with absorbent kitchen paper.
Add steak to wok and stir-fry for 4-5 minutes,
until browned on all sides. Remove and keep
warm.

Add mange tout (snow peas) and spring
onions to any oil remaining in wok and stir-
fry for 1 minute. Stir cornflour mixture and
stir into wok with reserved marinade and
bring to the boil. Add reserved noodles and
beef and chopped coriander. Toss to coat
well. Divide among 4 plates. Garnish with
coriander leaves and lime slices.

Serves 4.

BEEF STROGANOFF

2 tablespoons groundnut oil
800 g (1¾ lb) fillet or boneless sirloin steak, cut
    crosswise into 1 cm (½ in) strips
25 g (1 oz/2 tablespoons) butter
1 onion, thinly sliced
225 g (8 oz) mushrooms, thinly sliced
salt and freshly ground black pepper
1 tablespoon flour
115 ml (4 fl oz/½ cup) beef or veal stock
1 tablespoon Dijon mustard (optional)
250 ml (9 oz/1 cup) sour cream
pinch of cayenne pepper
dill sprigs, to garnish

Heat the wok until very hot. Add oil and
swirl to coat wok. Add half the beef strips.

Stir-fry for 1 minute until just browned and
still rare. With a slotted spoon, remove beef
to a bowl. Allow wok to reheat and add
remaining beef strips. Stir-fry for 1 minute
and turn beef and any juices into bowl. Add
butter to wok, then add onion. Reduce heat
to moderate and stir-fry onion for 3-4 minutes
until softened and beginning to colour. Add
mushrooms and increase heat; stir-fry for
2 minutes until mushrooms and onions are
softened and golden. Add salt and pepper and
stir in flour until well blended.

Add beef stock and bring to the boil, then
simmer for 1 minute until sauce thickens. Stir
in mustard, if using, and gradually add the
sour cream. (Do not allow sour cream to
boil.) Return beef strips and any juices to
sauce and cook gently for 1 minute until beef
is heated through. Sprinkle a little cayenne
pepper over and garnish with dill sprigs.
Serve with rice.

Serves 6.

—MEXICAN BEEF WITH BEANS—

450 g (1 lb) minced (ground) beef
1 onion, chopped
3-4 cloves garlic, finely chopped
1 green or red pepper (capsicum), diced
115 g (4 oz) can chopped green chillies, drained
425 g (15 oz) can red kidney beans, drained
320 g (11½ oz) can whole-kernel sweetcorn, drained
6 teaspoons chilli powder (or to taste)
2 teaspoons ground cumin
1 teaspoon dried oregano
800 g (28 oz) can peeled tomatoes
salt and freshly ground black pepper
3 tablespoons chopped fresh parsley
115 g (4 oz/1 cup) grated mature Cheddar cheese
chopped fresh parsley, to garnish

In the wok, place minced beef and heat until it begins to release juices. Increase heat and stir to break up meat and stir-fry for 5-6 minutes until meat is browned. Add onion, garlic, green or red pepper (capsicum), chopped chillies, kidney beans and sweetcorn and bring to the boil.

Stir in chilli powder, cumin, oregano and peeled tomatoes with their juice. Stir to break up tomatoes. Season with salt and pepper, lower heat and cook, covered, for 20-30 minutes until slightly thickened. Remove from heat, stir in the parsley and half the cheese. Sprinkle with remaining cheese and garnish with chopped parsley.

Serves 6-8.

ITALIAN BEEF SALAD

1 small head of escarole, Cos lettuce or other bitter
leaves, washed and dried thoroughly
2-3 tablespoons olive oil
450 g (1 lb) fillet steak, frozen for 20 minutes then cut
into very thin strips
8 anchovy fillets, sliced if large
55 g (2 oz) Parmesan cheese
2-4 tablespoons lemon juice
1 tablespoon capers, rinsed and drained
salt and freshly ground black pepper
chopped fresh herbs, to garnish

Arrange the escarole, Cos or other leaves on
4 large plates. Set aside.

Heat wok until very hot. Add 1 tablespoon
olive oil and a few beef strips. Fry 5-8 seconds
until beef just colours, turning each slice
once halfway through cooking. The beef
should be very rare. Remove to one of the
salad plates. Continue cooking beef in
batches, adding oil as necessary, and
arranging over leaves.

Place a few anchovy slices over the beef
slices. Using a swivel-bladed vegetable
peeler, shave paper-thin slices of Parmesan
cheese over the meat. Drizzle each salad with
lemon juice and sprinkle with capers. Season
with salt and pepper. Garnish with fresh
herbs.

Serves 4.

VEAL WITH PINE NUTS

225 g (8 oz) veal escalopes
3 tablespoons flour
salt and freshly ground black pepper
2 slices bacon, diced
55 g (2 oz/4 tablespoons) butter
2 tablespoons pine nuts
115 ml (4 fl oz/½ cup) dry white wine
1 tablespoon capers, drained
2 teaspoons shredded fresh sage leaves
fresh sage leaves, to garnish (optional)

Place escalopes between 2 sheets of grease-proof paper and pound to a 0.5 cm (¼ in) thickness. Cut veal into strips.

In a shallow dish combine flour with salt and pepper. Lightly dredge the veal strips, shaking off any excess flour. Place bacon in cold wok and heat over moderate heat until bacon begins to cook and melt. Increase heat and stir-fry for 1-2 minutes until bacon is crisp. Remove to a bowl. Add 1 teaspoon butter to drippings in wok and swirl to coat wok. Add pine nuts and stir-fry for 1 minute until golden. Remove to the bowl.

Add 1 tablespoon butter and the veal strips and stir-fry for 2-3 minutes until golden on all sides. Remove veal to 2 dinner plates and keep warm. Add wine to wok, stirring to deglaze and bring to the boil. Boil for 1-2 minutes until reduced by half, then stir in remaining butter. Add capers, bacon, pine nuts and sage and toss well. Season with pepper and spoon over veal. Garnish with sage leaves, if using. Serve with orzo (rice-shaped pasta) or linguine.

Serves 2.

— VEAL IN MUSTARD CREAM —

3 tablespoons flour
salt and cayenne pepper
225 g (8 oz) veal escalopes
1 tablespoon vegetable oil
15 g (½ oz/1 tablespoon) butter
2-3 shallots, thinly sliced
55 ml (2 fl oz/¼ cup) dry white wine
115 ml (4 fl oz/½ cup) whipping cream
2 tablespoons Dijon mustard
2 tablespoons fresh basil leaves or small dill sprigs with
    a few reserved for garnish

In a shallow dish, combine flour with salt and cayenne pepper to taste.

Place veal escalopes between 2 sheets of greaseproof paper and pound to a 0.5 cm (¼ in) thickness. Cut veal into strips. Lightly dredge the veal strips in flour, shaking off any excess. Heat the wok until very hot. Add the oil and swirl to coat wok. Add butter and swirl. Add veal strips and stir-fry for 2-3 minutes until golden on all sides. Remove veal to 2 dinner plates and keep warm.

Add the shallots to remaining oil in wok and cook for 2-3 minutes until softened. Add the white wine, stirring to deglaze, and bring to the boil. Boil for 1-2 minutes until reduced by half, then stir in cream and bring back to the boil. Cook for 1 minute more until sauce thickens slightly. Stir in the mustard and basil or dill. Pour sauce over veal and garnish with reserved leaves or sprigs. Serve with noodles or sautéed potatoes and a salad.

Serves 2.

— CALVES LIVER WITH BACON —

4 rashers bacon, cut into strips
1 onion, thinly sliced lengthwise into 'petals'
1 green dessert apple, cored and thinly sliced
salt and freshly ground black pepper
1 tablespoon vegetable oil
350 g (12 oz) calves liver, cut into thin strips
6 teaspoons cider vinegar
55 ml (2 fl oz/¼ cup) dry white wine or apple juice
2 teaspoons cornflour dissolved in 55 ml
    (2 fl oz/¼ cup) chicken stock or water
½ teaspoon dried thyme leaves
thyme sprigs or lemon wedges, to garnish

Place bacon in cold wok and heat over moderate heat until bacon begins to cook.

Increase heat and stir-fry for 1-2 minutes until bacon is crisp. Remove to a bowl. Add onion to dripping in wok and stir-fry for 1-2 minutes until just beginning to soften. Add apple slices and stir-fry for a further 1-2 minutes until apple begins to soften. Season with salt and pepper and remove to bowl. Add oil to wok and increase heat. Add liver strips and stir-fry for 1-2 minutes until just browned. The liver should be pink inside. Remove to bowl.

Stir cider vinegar into wok to deglaze, then stir in white wine or apple juice. Stir cornflour mixture and stir into wok with the thyme. Add reserved bacon, onion, apple and liver strips and cook for 1 minute until sauce bubbles and liver is heated through. Garnish with thyme sprigs or lemon wedges and serve with mashed or sautéed potatoes.

Serves 2.

- CHILLI-LAMB WITH TOMATOES -

1 tablespoon olive oil
4 lamb leg steaks or chump chops, about 175 g (6 oz)
    each, 1 cm (½ in) thick
2 cloves garlic, chopped
1 chilli, seeded and chopped
1 green pepper (capsicum), diced
1 courgette (zucchini), sliced
225 g (8 oz) red or red and yellow cherry tomatoes
50 g (2 oz/⅓ cup) sun-dried tomatoes in oil,
    drained and chopped
2 tablespoons bottled pesto sauce
fresh basil sprigs, to garnish

Heat the wok until very hot. Add the olive oil and swirl to coat.

Add the lamb steaks or chops and reduce heat slightly, then cook for 3-5 minutes until browned on both sides, turning once halfway through cooking. The lamb should be pink inside. Remove and keep warm. Pour off all but 1 tablespoon oil from wok and add garlic, chilli and pepper (capsicum). Stir-fry for 1 minute.

Add courgette (zucchini), cherry tomatoes, sun-dried tomatoes and pesto sauce and stir-fry for 3-4 minutes, until vegetables are tender but still crisp. Push vegetables aside and return lamb to wok. Cover lamb with vegetables and cook steaks or chops and vegetables together for 1 minute until flavours blend and lamb is heated through. Serve 1 or 2 steaks or chops per person garnished with basil.

Serves 2 or 4.

LAMB WITH SPINACH

3 tablespoons soy sauce
¼ teaspoon five-spice powder
2.5 cm (1 in) piece fresh root ginger, peeled and cut
   into julienne strips
2 cloves garlic, finely chopped
700 g (1½ lb) lamb fillet, cut crosswise into thin strips
1 tablespoon sesame oil
1 fresh red chilli, seeded and thinly sliced
8 spring onions, cut into 5 cm (2 in) pieces
1 mango, peeled and cut into 1 cm (½ in) thick pieces
175 g (6 oz) fresh baby spinach leaves,
   washed and dried
3 tablespoons dry sherry or rice wine
1 teaspoon cornflour dissolved in 1 tablespoon water

In a shallow baking dish, combine soy sauce, five-spice powder, ginger and garlic. Add lamb strips and toss to coat well. Leave to marinate for 1 hour, covered, stirring occasionally. Heat the wok until very hot. Add sesame oil and swirl to coat. With a slotted spoon and working in 2 batches, add lamb to wok, draining off and reserving as much marinade as possible. Stir-fry lamb for 2-3 minutes until browned on all sides. Remove to a bowl. Add chilli to oil remaining in wok and stir-fry for 1 minute.

Add spring onions and mango and stir-fry for 1 minute. Stir in spinach leaves, reserved lamb, dry sherry or rice wine and reserved marinade. Stir cornflour mixture and stir into wok. Stir-fry for 1 minute, tossing all ingredients until spinach wilts and lamb is lightly glazed with sauce. Serve with potatoes or noodles.

Serves 4.

ORANGE-GLAZED LAMB

1 tablespoon vegetable oil
700 g (1 ½ lb) lean lamb, cut into 1 cm (½ in) strips
150 ml (5 fl oz/⅔ cup) dry white wine
150 ml (5 fl oz/⅔ cup) freshly squeezed orange juice
1 teaspoon ground coriander
½ teaspoon dry mustard powder
salt and freshly ground black pepper
3 teaspoons cornflour dissolved in 2 tablespoons water
1 large orange, zest removed and cut into julienne
    strips, and flesh divided into segments
fresh mint, to garnish (optional)

Heat the wok until very hot. Add vegetable oil and swirl to coat wok.

Add lamb strips and stir-fry for 4-5 minutes. Remove to a plate and keep warm. Pour off all the fat from the wok and add the white wine, stirring to deglaze. Add orange juice, coriander, mustard powder, salt and pepper and bring to the boil. Stir the cornflour mixture and slowly pour into the wok, stirring constantly until sauce thickens.

Return the lamb strips to the sauce, turning to coat each one, and cook for 1-2 minutes until sauce has glazed the lamb strips and they are heated through. Add orange julienne and segments and cook for 1 minute to heat through. Arrange lamb and orange segments on 4 dinner plates and garnish with mint, if wished. Serve with green beans.

Serves 4.

MEXICAN-STYLE LAMB

115 ml (4 fl oz/½ cup) dry white wine
115 ml (4 fl oz/½ cup) pineapple juice
2-4 tablespoons lime or lemon juice
8 tablespoons chopped fresh coriander
3 chillies, seeded and chopped
2 cloves garlic, finely chopped
700 g (1½ lb) lamb fillet, cut crosswise into thin strips
1 large avocado
1 large tomato, peeled, seeded and chopped
1 Cos lettuce, shredded
2 tablespoons vegetable oil
1 onion, sliced
6 warm tortillas or pitta breads, to serve (optional)

In a medium bowl, combine 1 tablespoon each of wine, pineapple juice and lime or lemon juice, 2 tablespoons of coriander, one of chopped chillies and half the chopped garlic. Set aside. Combine the remainder of these ingredients in a shallow baking dish and add the lamb strips. Toss to coat then marinate, covered, for 1 hour. Peel and chop the avocado and add to the first bowl with the chopped tomato. Toss to blend ingredients. Arrange lettuce around edge of a serving plate, spoon avocado mixture on top and set aside.

Heat the wok until very hot. Add the oil and swirl to coat. With a slotted spoon, remove lamb strips from marinade and add to wok in 2 batches and stir-fry for 2-3 minutes until browned. Remove to a bowl. Add onion to the wok and stir-fry for 2-3 minutes until softened. Return lamb and any juices to the wok. Cook for 1 minute until lamb is heated through. Spoon lamb onto centre of serving dish and serve with warm tortillas or pitta bread, if wished.

Serves 6.

STIR-FRIED MOUSSAKA

1 tablespoon olive oil
2 onions, chopped
2 cloves garlic, chopped
700 g (1½ lb) lean minced (ground) lamb
400 g (14 oz) can chopped or crushed tomatoes
3-4 courgettes (zucchini), sliced into 1 cm
    (½ in) pieces
1 tablespoon capers, rinsed and drained
2 tablespoons chopped fresh oregano or basil or
    1 tablespoon dried oregano or basil
salt and freshly ground black pepper
300 g (10 oz/1½ cups) orzo (rice-shaped pasta)
115 g (4 oz/1 cup) feta cheese, crumbled

Heat the wok until hot. Add oil and swirl to
coat wok. Add onions and garlic and stir-fry
for 2-3 minutes until softened. Add lamb and
stir-fry for 4-5 minutes until browned.

Add tomatoes, courgettes (zucchini), capers,
oregano or basil and salt and pepper. Stir in
350 ml (12 fl oz/1½ cups) water and the orzo
and bring to the boil. Reduce heat to low and
cook, covered, for 8-10 minutes until orzo is
cooked and most of the liquid absorbed.
Remove wok from heat and stir in the feta
cheese. Serve with a green salad and crusty
bread.

Serves 6-8.

── PORK & PRUNE MEDLEY ──

450 g (1 lb) pork fillet, cut into thin slices
2 tablespoons soy sauce
6 teaspoons balsamic or cider vinegar
2 tablespoons olive oil
2 courgettes (zucchini), sliced
1 onion, cut lengthwise into 'petals'
1 red pepper (capsicum), cut into thin strips
115 g (4 oz) mushrooms, sliced
115 g (4 oz) mange tout (snow peas)
115 g (4 oz) asparagus, cut into 5 cm (2 in) pieces
55 g (2 oz/½ cup) walnut halves
175 g (6 oz) ready-to-eat prunes, stoned
salt and freshly ground black pepper

In a shallow baking dish, sprinkle pork slices with soy sauce and balsamic or cider vinegar and toss to coat well. Allow to stand for 30 minutes. Heat the wok until hot. Add olive oil and swirl to coat wok. Add pork slices and stir-fry for 3-5 minutes, until golden on all sides. With a slotted spoon, remove to a bowl.

Add courgettes (zucchini), onion, red pepper (capsicum), mushrooms, mange tout (snow peas), asparagus, walnut halves and prunes and stir-fry for 2-3 minutes until well coated with oil. Add 2 tablespoons water to wok and cover wok quickly. Steam for 1-2 minutes until vegetables just begin to soften. Uncover wok, return pork to wok and toss to mix. Season with salt and pepper. Stir-fry for a further 1-2 minutes until pork is heated through.

Serves 4.

— COCONUT PORK WITH LIME —

6 pork escalopes, about 115 g (4 oz) each
1 cm (½ in) piece fresh root ginger, peeled and grated
2 teaspoons ground cumin
1 teaspoon ground coriander
1 teaspoon chilli powder (to taste)
1 teaspoon paprika
½ teaspoon salt
2-3 tablespoons vegetable oil
1 onion, cut lengthwise in half and thinly sliced
3-4 cloves garlic, finely chopped
300 ml (10 fl oz/1¼ cups) unsweetened coconut milk
grated rind and juice of 1 large lime
1 small Chinese cabbage, shredded
lime slices and coriander leaves, to garnish

Place escalopes between 2 sheets of grease-proof paper. Pound to a 0.5 cm (¼ in) thickness. Cut into strips. In a large, shallow dish, combine ginger, cumin, coriander, chilli powder, paprika and salt. Stir in pork strips and leave to stand for 15 minutes. Heat wok until very hot. Add half the oil and swirl to coat wok. Add half the pork and stir-fry for 2-3 minutes. Remove to a plate and keep warm. Cook remaining strips using remaining oil. Keep warm. Pour off all but 1 tablespoon oil from the wok.

Add onion and garlic to wok; stir-fry for 2-3 minutes until onion is softened. Slowly add coconut milk. Bring to simmering point but do not boil. Stir in lime rind and juice and shredded cabbage. Simmer gently for 5-7 minutes, stirring frequently, until cabbage is tender and sauce slightly thickened. Add pork and cook, covered, for 1-2 minutes until heated through. Arrange pork and cabbage on plates and garnish with lime slices and coriander. Serve with noodles.

Serves 6.

─── RATATOUILLE-STYLE PORK ───

1 tablespoon olive oil
4 boneless loin pork chops, about 575 g (1 ¼ lb) and
   2.5 cm (1 in) thick, trimmed of fat
1 onion, coarsely chopped
2 cloves garlic, chopped
1 small aubergine (eggplant), cut into 2.5 cm
   (1 in) cubes
1 red or green pepper (capsicum), diced
2 courgettes (zucchini), thickly sliced
225 g (8 oz) can chopped tomatoes
1 teaspoon chopped fresh oregano or basil leaves or
   ½ teaspoon dried oregano or basil
½ teaspoon dried thyme leaves
salt and freshly ground black pepper
fresh parsley or coriander sprigs, to garnish

Heat the wok until very hot. Add olive oil and swirl to coat. Arrange pork chops on bottom and side of wok, if necessary, in a single layer. Fry for 4-5 minutes until well browned on both sides, turning once and rotating during cooking. Remove to a plate. Add onion and garlic to remaining oil in wok and stir-fry for 1 minute until onion begins to soften. Add the aubergine (eggplant) cubes and diced pepper (capsicum) and stir-fry for 3-5 minutes to brown and soften.

Add courgettes (zucchini), chopped tomatoes and their juice, the fresh or dried oregano or basil, thyme and season with salt and pepper. Stir well and return pork chops to wok, covering them with the ratatouille mixture. Lower the heat and cook, covered, for 6-8 minutes, shaking wok occasionally to prevent sticking. Uncover and cook for 2-3 minutes more to allow sauce to thicken slightly. Garnish with parsley or coriander. Serve with fresh pasta.

Serves 4.

—— INDONESIAN-STYLE PORK ——

1 tablespoon seasoned flour
575 g (1¼ lb) pork fillet, cut into small cubes
2-3 tablespoons vegetable oil
1 onion, cut lengthwise in half and thinly sliced
2 cloves garlic, finely chopped
2.5 cm (1 in) piece fresh root ginger, peeled and
    cut into julienne strips
½ teaspoon sambal oelek (see Note) or
    Chinese chilli sauce
55 ml (2 fl oz/¼ cup) Indonesian soy sauce or dark soy
    sauce sweetened with 1 tablespoon sugar
coriander leaves, to garnish

In a medium bowl, combine seasoned flour
and pork cubes and toss to coat well. Shake to
remove any excess flour.

Heat the wok until very hot. Add 2 tablespoons of the oil and swirl to coat wok. Add
pork cubes and stir-fry for 3-4 minutes until
browned on all sides, adding a little more oil
if necessary. Push pork to one side and add
onion, garlic and ginger and stir-fry for 1
minute, tossing all the ingredients.

Add sambal oelek or chilli sauce, soy sauce
and 150 ml (5 fl oz/⅔ cup) water; stir. Bring
to the boil, then reduce heat to low and
simmer gently, covered, for 20-25 minutes,
stirring occasionally, until pork is tender and
sauce thickened. Garnish with coriander and
serve with fried rice or noodles.

Serves 4.

Note: Sambal oelek is a very hot, chilli-based
Indonesian condiment available in specialist
or oriental food shops.

– PORK WITH MELON & MANGO –

1 small Galia or ½ Honeydew melon, cut into
    julienne strips
1 slightly under-ripe mango, peeled and cut into
    julienne strips
salt and freshly ground black pepper
1 tablespoon sugar
juice of 1 lime or lemon
2 tablespoons sesame oil
225 g (8 oz) pork fillet, cut into shreds
4-6 spring onions, thinly sliced
2 cloves garlic, finely chopped
5 tablespoons nam pla (fish sauce)
1 tablespoon cider vinegar
½ teaspoon crushed chillies
chopped peanuts and chopped coriander, to garnish

In a medium bowl, toss melon and mango
strips with the salt and pepper to taste, sugar
and lime or lemon juice. Set aside. Heat the
wok until very hot. Add oil and swirl to coat,
add shredded pork and stir-fry for 2-3 minutes
until golden. With a slotted spoon, remove
to absorbent kitchen paper and drain.

To the oil remaining in the wok, add spring
onions and garlic and stir-fry for 1 minute.
Stir in the nam pla (fish sauce), vinegar and
chillies and salt and pepper if necessary. Add
the reserved pork and melon and mango,
together with any juices. Toss to mix ingredients and heat through. Spoon onto a
shallow serving dish and sprinkle with
chopped peanuts and coriander. Serve hot
or warm with noodles or shredded Chinese
cabbage.

Serves 2.

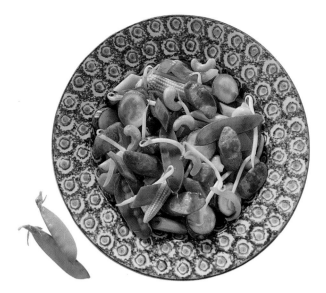

— CHINESE SAUSAGE STIR-FRY —

2 tablespoons sesame or vegetable oil
225 g (8 oz) Chinese sausage (see Note) or sweet
   Italian-style sausage, cut diagonally into thin slices
1 onion, cut in half lengthwise and sliced
1 red pepper (capsicum), diced
115 g (4 oz) baby sweetcorn
2 courgettes (zucchini), thinly sliced
115 g (4 oz) mange tout (snow peas)
8 spring onions, cut into 2.5 cm (1 in) pieces
25 g (1 oz) beansprouts, rinsed and drained
25 g (1 oz/¼ cup) cashew nuts or peanuts
2 tablespoons soy sauce
3 tablespoons dry sherry or rice wine

Heat the wok until hot. Add sesame or vegetable oil and swirl to coat wok. Add sausage slices and stir-fry for 3-4 minutes until browned and cooked. Add onion, pepper and sweetcorn and stir-fry for 3 minutes. Add courgettes (zucchini), mange tout (snow peas) and spring onions and stir-fry for a further 2 minutes.

Stir in the beansprouts and nuts and stir-fry for 1-2 minutes. Add soy sauce and dry sherry or rice wine and stir-fry for 1 minute until vegetables are tender but still crisp and sausage slices completely cooked through. Serve with rice or noodles.

Serve 4.

Note: Chinese sausage is available in Chinese groceries and some specialist shops and needs cooking before being used.

SAUSAGE & PEPPERS

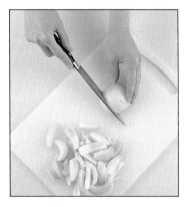

2 tablespoons olive oil
700 g (1 ½ lb) hot, sweet or mixed Italian sausages
2 onions, halved lengthwise, then cut lengthwise
  into 'petals'
4-6 cloves garlic, finely chopped
1 each large red, green and yellow pepper (capsicum),
  cut in half lengthwise then into strips
225 g (8 oz) can peeled tomatoes
1 tablespoon fresh shredded oregano or basil or
  1 teaspoon dried oregano or basil
½ teaspoon crushed chillies
½ teaspoon dried thyme
½ teaspoon rubbed sage
salt and freshly ground black pepper
fresh oregano or basil leaves, to garnish
Parmesan cheese, to serve

Heat the wok until hot. Add olive oil and
swirl to coat wok. Add sausages and cook
over moderate heat for 8-10 minutes until
sausages are golden brown on all sides, turning and rotating sausages frequently during
cooking. Remove sausages to a plate and pour
off all but 2 tablespoons oil from the wok.
Add onions and garlic and stir-fry for 2
minutes until golden. Add the red, green and
yellow pepper (capsicum) strips and stir-fry
for 1-2 minutes until just beginning to soften.

Add tomatoes and their liquid, fresh or dried
oregano or basil, crushed chillies, thyme,
sage, salt and pepper. Stir to break up the
tomatoes and mix well. Return sausages to
wok and cover with the vegetable mixture.
Simmer for 15-20 minutes until vegetables
are tender and sauce is thickened. Garnish
with fresh oregano or basil leaves and sprinkle
with shaved or grated Parmesan cheese.
Serve with saffron rice or spaghetti.

Serves 6.

──PORK WITH CHILLI & PEAS──

450 g (1 lb) pork fillet, cut crosswise into thin slices
1 ½ tablespoons soy sauce
6 teaspoons cider vinegar
1 tablespoon vegetable oil
2.5 cm (1 in) piece fresh root ginger, peeled and
    finely chopped
2 cloves garlic, finely chopped
1 fresh red chilli, seeded and thinly sliced
225 g (8 oz) fresh or frozen green peas or
    sugar snap peas
85 g (3 oz) red cabbage or radicchio, thinly shredded

In a small baking dish, sprinkle pork slices
with soy sauce and vinegar. Toss to coat well.
Leave to stand for 15-20 minutes.

Heat the wok until hot. Add oil and swirl to
coat wok. Add pork slices and stir-fry for
2 minutes. Push to one side and add ginger,
garlic and chilli; stir-fry for 1 minute to mix.

Add peas or sugar snap peas and red cabbage
or radicchio and stir-fry for 2-3 minutes until
vegetables are tender but still crisp. Serve
with rice and wild rice.

Serves 4.

— PORK ESCALOPES NORMAND —

4 pork escalopes about 575 g (1¼ lb), 1 cm
  (½ in) thick
2 tablespoons vegetable oil
25 g (1 oz/2 tablespoons) butter
1 clove garlic, chopped
2 dessert apples, halved lengthwise, cored and thinly
  sliced
½ teaspoon dried thyme
3 tablespoons Calvados or brandy
115 ml (4 fl oz/½ cup) double or whipping cream
salt and freshly ground black pepper
apple slices and parsley sprigs, to garnish

Place pork escalopes between 2 sheets of
greaseproof paper and pound to a 0.5 cm
(¼ in) thickness. Cut into thin strips.

Heat the wok until very hot. Add oil and
swirl to coat wok. Add half the pork strips
and stir-fry for 2-3 minutes until golden on all
sides. Remove to a plate, keep warm, and
cook the remaining strips in the same way.
Pour off any oil from the wok. Add butter to
the wok and allow to melt. Add garlic, apple
slices and thyme and stir-fry for 1-2 minutes
until apple slices are golden.

Add Calvados or brandy to the wok and stir
to deglaze. Add cream and bring to the boil.
Add salt and pepper to taste. Cook for 1
minute, stirring constantly, until sauce
thickens slightly and apples are tender.
Arrange pork strips on 4 dinner plates and
spoon over apples and sauce. Garnish with
apple slices and parsley sprigs. Serve with
buttered egg noodles or sautéed potatoes.

Serves 4.

─────── PORK WITH BASIL ───────

250 g (9 oz) thin egg noodles
55 ml (2 fl oz/¼ cup) olive oil
575 g (1¼ lb) pork fillet, cut into shreds
1 red onion, cut lengthwise in half, and thinly sliced
4 tablespoons shredded fresh basil leaves
6 teaspoons balsamic vinegar
3 tablespoons toasted pine nuts
salt and freshly ground black pepper
fresh basil leaves, to garnish

In a large saucepan of boiling water, cook the egg noodles according to the packet directions. Drain and rinse. Turn into a large bowl and toss with 2 tablespoons olive oil. Keep warm.

Heat the wok until very hot. Add remaining olive oil and swirl to coat wok. Add shredded pork and stir-fry for 2-3 minutes until pork is golden. Add red onion and toss with the pork, then stir-fry for 1 minute.

Stir in shredded basil, the balsamic vinegar and pine nuts and toss to mix well. Add noodles to the wok, season to taste and toss with pork mixture. Turn onto shallow serving dish and garnish with basil leaves.

Serves 4.

— SPICY PORK BALLS & TOFU —

350 g (12 oz) lean minced pork
1 egg white
3-6 teaspoons chilli sauce
½ teaspoon ground turmeric
salt
3 tablespoons vegetable oil
225 g (8 oz) firm tofu (bean curd), drained and cubed
1 red pepper (capsicum), diced
225 g (8 oz) green beans, cut into 2.5 cm (1 in) pieces
2 cloves garlic, finely chopped
2.5 cm (1 in) piece fresh root ginger, peeled and
    finely chopped
2 teaspoons cornflour
115 ml (4 fl oz/½ cup) chicken stock
coriander sprigs, to garnish

In a bowl, combine minced pork, egg white, ½ teaspoon chilli sauce, turmeric and salt. Mix well. With hands, form into 16 small balls. Refrigerate for 25-30 minutes to firm. Heat the wok until hot. Add 2 tablespoons oil and, working in 2 batches, add the pork balls. Stir-fry for 3-4 minutes until golden on all sides. Remove balls to absorbent kitchen paper to drain; keep warm. Add tofu (bean curd) cubes to wok and stir-fry gently for 2-3 minutes, being careful tofu does not break up. With a slotted spoon, remove to absorbent kitchen paper to drain.

Add remaining oil to wok. Add pepper and beans and stir-fry for 3-4 minutes. Remove to a bowl. Add garlic and ginger and stir-fry for 1 minute. Dissolve cornflour in chicken stock and stir into wok. Add remaining chilli sauce, to taste, and simmer, stirring for 1 minute. Return pork to wok and simmer, covered, for 8-10 minutes. Uncover and add tofu (bean curd), pepper (capsicum) and green beans. Cook gently for 1-2 minutes. Garnish and serve with rice.

Serves 4.

——— HAM & PLUM STIR-FRY ———

2 tablespoons vegetable oil
1 red pepper (capsicum), cut lengthwise in half,
   thinly sliced
350 g (12 oz) plums or nectarines, stoned, thinly sliced
225 g (8 oz) oyster mushrooms, sliced
2 leeks, trimmed, washed and cut diagonally into
   1 cm (½ in) pieces
6 spring onions, thinly sliced
450 g (1 lb) gammon steaks, cut into 2.5 cm
   (1 in) strips
250 ml (9 fl oz/1 cup) orange juice
2 tablespoons peach or apricot preserve
2 tablespoons soy sauce
6 teaspoons wine vinegar
2 teaspoons cornflour dissolved in 2 tablespoons water

Heat the wok until hot. Add oil and swirl to coat wok. Add red pepper (capsicum), plums or nectarines and stir-fry for 1-2 minutes. Add oyster mushrooms and leeks and stir-fry for 1-2 minutes until vegetables begin to soften. Push vegetables to one side and add spring onions and gammon strips. Stir-fry for 2-3 minutes, tossing ingredients to mix, until gammon is heated through.

Stir in orange juice, peach or apricot preserve, soy sauce and vinegar. Stir the cornflour mixture, then stir into wok. Bring to the boil and stir-fry for 1-2 minutes until sauce thickens and coats ingredients. Serve with rice or noodles.

Serve 4-6.

—— SZECHUAN AUBERGINE ——

450 g (1 lb) small aubergines (eggplants), cut into
   2.5 cm (1 in) cubes or thin slices
salt
2 tablespoons groundnut oil
2 cloves garlic, finely chopped
2.5 cm (1 in) piece fresh root ginger, peeled and
   finely chopped
3-4 spring onions, finely sliced
2 tablespoons dark soy sauce
3-6 teaspoons chilli bean paste or sauce or 1 teaspoon
   crushed dried chillies
1 tablespoon yellow bean paste (optional)
2 tablespoons dry sherry or rice wine
3 teaspoons cider vinegar
1 tablespoon sugar
chopped fresh parsley, to garnish

Place aubergine (eggplant) cubes in a plastic
or stainless steel colander or sieve, placed on
a plate or baking sheet. Sprinkle with salt and
leave to stand 30 minutes. Rinse aubergine
(eggplant) under cold running water and turn
out onto layers of absorbent kitchen paper;
pat dry thoroughly. Heat wok until very hot.
Add oil and swirl to coat wok. Add garlic,
ginger and spring onions and stir-fry for
1-2 minutes until spring onions begin to
soften. Add aubergine (eggplant) and stir-fry
for 2-3 minutes until softened and beginning
to brown.

Stir in remaining ingredients and 150 ml
(5 fl oz/2/3 cup) water and bring to the boil.
Reduce the heat and simmer for 5-7 minutes
until aubergine (eggplant) is very tender, stirring frequently. Increase heat to high and
stir-fry mixture until the liquid is almost
completely reduced. Spoon into serving dish
and garnish with parsley.

Serves 4-6.

-GINGERED BRUSSELS SPROUTS-

3 tablespoons vegetable oil
1 onion, cut lengthwise in half and thinly sliced
1-2 cloves garlic, finely chopped
2.5 cm (1 in) piece fresh root ginger, peeled and cut
   into julienne strips
1 kg (2 lb) Brussels sprouts, washed, trimmed
   and shredded
1 tablespoon crystallized ginger, chopped, or
   1 piece stem ginger in syrup, chopped
salt and cayenne pepper

Heat the wok until hot. Add oil and swirl to coat wok. Add onion, garlic and ginger and stir-fry for 1 minute. Add remaining oil. Stir in the shredded sprouts and crystallized or stem ginger and stir-fry for 2-3 minutes.

Add 2 tablespoons water and cook, covered, for 2-3 minutes, stirring once or twice. Uncover and add 1 tablespoon water if sprouts seem too dry. Stir in salt and cayenne pepper and turn into a serving dish.

Serves 4-6.

SPICY CAULIFLOWER

55 g (2 oz/¼ cup) whole almonds
1 large cauliflower, divided into flowerets
55 g (2 oz/4 tablespoons) butter
1 onion, finely chopped
½ teaspoon chilli powder
½ teaspoon turmeric
3-4 tablespoons lemon juice
55 g (2 oz/½ cup) dried breadcrumbs
salt and freshly ground black pepper
lime wedges and parsley sprigs, to garnish

Heat the wok until hot. Add the almonds and stir-fry over a moderate heat until browned on all sides. Remove to a plate. When cool, chop almonds coarsely.

Half-fill the wok with water and over high heat bring to the boil. Add the cauliflower pieces and simmer for 2 minutes. Drain and rinse; set aside. Wipe wok dry and return to heat. Add butter to wok and swirl until melted. Add the onion, chilli powder and turmeric and stir-fry for 2-3 minutes until softened.

Add the blanched cauliflower pieces and lemon juice and stir-fry for 3-4 minutes until tender but still crisp. Add the breadcrumbs and chopped almonds and toss until cauliflower pieces are well coated. Season with salt and pepper. Turn into a serving dish and serve hot, garnished with lime wedges and parsley.

Serves 4-6.

-BOMBAY POTATOES WITH PEAS-

55 ml (2 fl oz/¼ cup) vegetable oil
1 onion, finely chopped
2 cloves garlic, finely chopped
1 teaspoon whole cumin seeds
1 teaspoon black mustard seeds
3 teaspoons medium curry powder
½ teaspoon ground cardamom
450 g (1 lb) potatoes, cut into 1 cm (½ in) pieces and
    boiled until just tender
175 g (6 oz) fresh or frozen peas
1-2 tablespoons lemon juice
2 tablespoons chopped fresh coriander
coriander sprigs, to garnish

Heat the wok until hot. Add oil and swirl to coat wok. Add onion and garlic and reduce heat to medium. Stir-fry for 4-6 minutes until onion is tender and golden. Add the cumin seeds and black mustard seeds and stir-fry for 2 minutes until seeds begin to pop. Stir in the curry powder and ground cardamom and stir-fry for a further 2-3 minutes.

Add potatoes and peas and stir-fry, tossing to coat with the spice mixture, for 2-3 minutes. Add lemon juice and chopped coriander and toss gently until potatoes and peas are well coated and heated through, adding a little water if potatoes begin to stick. Serve hot, garnished with coriander sprigs.

Serves 4-6.

— SWEET & SOUR VEGETABLES —

5 teaspoons cornflour
427 g (15½ oz) can pineapple chunks in natural juice,
    drained, juice reserved
3-4 tablespoons light brown sugar, or to taste
70 ml (2½ fl oz/⅓ cup) cider vinegar
2 tablespoons soy sauce
2 tablespoons dry sherry or rice wine
55 ml (2 fl oz/¼ cup) tomato ketchup (sauce)
2 tablespoons vegetable oil
2 carrots, thinly sliced
1 red pepper (capsicum), cut lengthwise in half and
    thinly sliced
1 fennel bulb, trimmed, thinly sliced
175 g (6 oz) baby corn, trimmed
175 g (6 oz) mange tout (snow peas) or sugar snap peas
175 g (6 oz) courgettes (zucchini), thinly sliced

In a small bowl, dissolve the cornflour in the reserved pineapple juice. Stir in brown sugar, vinegar, soy sauce, dry sherry or rice wine and tomato ketchup (sauce) until well blended. Set aside.

Heat the wok until very hot. Add vegetable oil and swirl to coat wok. Add carrots, pepper (capsicum) slices and fennel and stir-fry for 3-4 minutes until carrots just begin to soften. Stir the cornflour mixture and stir into wok. Bring to the boil and stir until sauce bubbles and thickens. Add baby corn, mange tout (snow peas) or sugar snap peas and courgettes (zucchini) and simmer for 1-2 minutes. Stir in reserved pineapple chunks and toss for 30 seconds. Spoon into serving dish.

Serves 4.

──CARROTS & MANGE TOUT──

3 tablespoons vegetable oil
350 g (12 oz) carrots, thinly sliced
1 bulb fennel, thinly sliced
175 g (6 oz) mange tout (snow peas) or sugar snap peas
4-6 spring onions, thinly sliced
115 ml (4 fl oz/½ cup) orange juice
grated rind of 1 orange, segments and juice reserved
2-3 tablespoons orange liqueur (optional)
1 tablespoon brown sugar
½ teaspoon ground cinnamon
25 g (1 oz/2 tablespoons) butter, cut into small pieces

Heat wok until hot. Add oil and swirl to coat. Add carrots and stir-fry for 3 minutes.

Add fennel and mange tout (snow peas) and stir-fry for a further 2-3 minutes until vegetables are tender but still crisp. Remove to a bowl. Add spring onions to remaining oil in the wok and stir-fry for 30 seconds. Add orange juice plus any juice from the segmented orange, orange liqueur, if using, brown sugar, cinnamon and orange rind. Increase heat to high and bring to the boil. Boil for 2-3 minutes until slightly thickened and reduced by about half.

Gradually stir in the butter until a smooth sauce forms. Add the reserved vegetables and toss to coat with sauce. Stir-fry for 30-45 seconds until heated through. Add orange segments, stir gently to mix and turn into serving dish. Serve hot.

Serves 6.

— WOK-SAUTÉED POTATOES —

2 tablespoons olive oil
25 g (1 oz/2 tablespoons) butter
4 slices streaky smoked bacon, diced
1 onion, sliced
1 clove garlic, finely chopped
700 g - 1 kg (1 ½ - 2 lb) old potatoes, cooked, peeled and
    cut into 1 cm (½ in) slices
1 tablespoon chopped fresh rosemary or thyme or
    1 teaspoon dried rosemary or thyme
2-3 tablespoons balsamic or fruit-flavour wine vinegar
salt and freshly ground black pepper
chopped fresh rosemary, to garnish (optional)

Heat the wok until hot. Add olive oil and butter and swirl to coat. Add bacon and stir-fry for 2 minutes until crisp. Add onion and garlic and stir-fry for 2-3 minutes until browned and beginning to soften.

Add the potato slices and rosemary or thyme and toss to combine. Cook gently for 3-5 minutes, stirring occasionally until potatoes are browned and crisp. Add vinegar to taste and season with salt and pepper. Garnish with extra chopped rosemary, if wished. Turn into serving bowl.

Serves 6.

—CREAMY CUCUMBER & LEEKS—

25 g (1 oz/2 tablespoons) butter
1 cucumber, about 450 g (1 lb), lightly peeled, seeded
  and cut into 5 cm (2 in) julienne strips
2 leeks, about 350 g (12 oz), trimmed, washed and cut
  into 5 cm (2 in) julienne strips
1 clove garlic, finely chopped
3-4 tablespoons dry sherry or white wine
115 ml (4 fl oz/½ cup) double (heavy) or whipping
  cream
3 tablespoons chopped fresh dill
salt and freshly ground black pepper
dill sprigs, to garnish

Heat the wok until hot. Add butter and swirl until butter melts. Add cucumber and leek strips and garlic and stir-fry for 2-3 minutes until cucumber strips begin to turn translucent. Add the sherry or wine and continue stir-frying for 1 minute until liquid has evaporated.

Add the cream and toss cucumber and leeks for 1-2 minutes until well coated with the cream and tender but still crisp. Stir in the chopped dill and season with salt and pepper. Turn into a serving dish and serve hot, garnished with dill sprigs.

Serves 4-6.

— GREEK-STYLE VEGETABLES —

CHERRY TOMATO STIR-FRY
2 tablespoons olive oil
1 clove garlic, finely chopped
350 g (12 oz) red and yellow cherry tomatoes
4 spring onions, thinly sliced
55 g (2 oz/¼ cup) toasted pine nuts
2 tablespoons chopped fresh basil plus herbs, to garnish
1 tablespoon balsamic or red wine vinegar
freshly ground black pepper

Heat wok until hot. Add oil and swirl to coat. Add garlic and tomatoes and stir-fry for 2-4 minutes until tomato skins crinkle. Add the onions, nuts, basil and vinegar. Stir-fry for 1 minute; season. Garnish and serve.

BROAD BEANS GREEK-STYLE
700 g (1½ lb) broad beans, shelled
2 tablespoons olive oil
1 clove garlic
½ teaspoon dried oregano or basil
½ teaspoon sugar
1 teaspoon white wine vinegar
55 g (2 oz) feta cheese, crumbled
fresh oregano or basil leaves, to garnish

Place beans in wok and add water to cover. Bring to the boil and simmer for 1 minute. Drain and rinse beans under cold running water. With fingers, slip beans out of outer skins and set aside. Dry wok.

Heat wok until hot. Add olive oil and swirl to coat. Add garlic and stir-fry for 5-10 seconds, then remove and discard. Add beans, dried oregano or basil and sugar and stir-fry for 3-4 minutes over moderate heat until beans are tender. Stir in wine vinegar. Remove from heat and toss with crumbled feta cheese. Garnish with oregano or basil leaves. Serve hot or warm.

Serves 4.

- MEDITERRANEAN VEGETABLES -

ASPARAGUS WITH RADISHES
2-3 tablespoons olive oil
700 g (1½ lb) thin asparagus, trimmed and cut into
    5-7.5 cm (2-3 in) pieces
8 large radishes, washed, trimmed and thinly sliced
4-6 spring onions, sliced
2 tablespoons balsamic or cider vinegar (optional)

Heat wok until very hot. Add oil and swirl to
coat wok. Add asparagus pieces and stir-fry for
2-3 minutes. Add radishes and spring onions
and stir-fry for 1-2 minutes until asparagus
is tender but still crisp. Add balsamic or
cider vinegar, if using, and toss to coat.

COURGETTES WITH PARMA HAM
2 tablespoons vegetable oil
800 g (1¾ lb) courgettes (zucchini), cut into 5 cm
    (2 in) julienne strips
1 red pepper (capsicum), cut into julienne strips
55 ml (2 fl oz/¼ cup) light soy sauce
3-4 tablespoons rice wine or cider vinegar
1 tablespoon brown sugar
1 tablespoon sesame oil
55 g (2 oz) sliced Parma ham, shredded
chopped chives, to garnish

Heat the wok until hot. Add vegetable oil
and swirl to coat. Add courgettes (zucchini)
and red pepper (capsicum) and stir-fry for
3-4 minutes until vegetables are tender but
still crisp. Stir in soy sauce, rice wine or cider
vinegar and brown sugar and toss to dissolve
sugar. Add sesame oil and shredded ham and
toss to mix. Serve garnished with chives.

Serves 6.

SPICY VEGETABLES

AROMATIC CABBAGE

55 ml (2 fl oz/¼ cup) vegetable oil
2 cloves garlic, finely chopped
2 tablespoons raisins
1 red pepper (capsicum), very thinly sliced
1 teaspoon Chinese chilli sauce
6-8 spring onions, thinly sliced
6-9 teaspoons lemon juice
1 Savoy or Chinese cabbage, thinly shredded

Heat wok until hot. Add oil and swirl to coat.
Add garlic, raisins and pepper (capsicum)
and stir-fry for 2 minutes. Stir in the chilli
sauce, spring onions and lemon juice; toss.
Add cabbage and stir-fry for 3-5 minutes.

CHILLI-ALMOND COURGETTES

2 tablespoons vegetable oil
2-3 cloves garlic, finely chopped
2.5 cm (1 in) piece fresh root ginger, peeled and
    finely chopped
½ teaspoon chilli powder
1 teaspoon sweet Chinese chilli sauce (to taste)
½ teaspoon sugar
700 g (1½ lb) mixed green and yellow courgettes
    (zucchini), cut into 2.5 cm (1 in) pieces

Heat the wok until hot. Add the oil and swirl
to coat. Add the garlic and ginger and stir-fry
for 1 minute. Stir in the chilli powder, chilli
sauce and sugar.

Add the courgettes (zucchini) and toss to
coat with flavourings. Stir in 2 tablespoons
water and stir-fry for 3-5 minutes until tender
but still crisp, adding a little more water if
necessary. Serve hot or at room temperature.

Serves 4-6.

—— WARM ANTIPASTI SALAD ——

mixed salad leaves, such as red leaf lettuce, escarole,
  radicchio and rocket, to serve
5 tablespoons olive oil
9 teaspoons red wine or balsamic vinegar
400 g (14 oz) can artichoke hearts, rinsed and drained,
  cut in half if large
225 g (8 oz) can cannellini beans, rinsed and drained
1 clove garlic, chopped
1 red onion, chopped
½ teaspoon dried basil
200 g (7 oz) jar roasted sweet red peppers (pimientos),
  drained and cut into 1 cm (½ in) strips
4 sun-dried tomatoes, drained and cut into thin strips
1 tablespoon capers, rinsed and drained
85 g (3 oz) black olives
fresh basil leaves (optional)

In a large bowl, toss the salad leaves with 3
tablespoons olive oil and 6 teaspoons vinegar. Arrange the mixed salad leaves on a
large, shallow serving dish. Heat the wok
until hot. Add the remaining oil and swirl to
coat. Add the artichoke hearts, cannellini
beans, garlic, red onion and basil and stir-fry
for 2-3 minutes until heated through. Carefully spoon the mixture onto the salad leaves.

Add the red peppers and sun-dried tomatoes
to wok and toss gently for 1-2 minutes to heat
through. Arrange over the artichoke and bean
mixture. Sprinkle with the capers, black
olives and basil leaves, if wished, and serve
warm with crusty bread.

Serves 4-6.

—— WILTED SPINACH SALAD ——

450 g (1 lb) baby spinach leaves
3 tablespoons olive oil
6 slices bacon, diced
1 fennel bulb, thinly sliced
225 g (8 oz) mushrooms, quartered
4-6 spring onions, thinly sliced
6 teaspoons cider vinegar
3 teaspoons Dijon mustard
1 teaspoon sugar
freshly ground black pepper
lemon and radish slices, to garnish (optional)

Arrange spinach leaves in a large bowl, tearing any large leaves into smaller pieces if necessary.

Heat the wok until hot. Add oil and swirl to coat. Add bacon and stir-fry for 2-3 minutes until bacon is just golden and crisp. Add fennel and mushrooms and stir-fry for 2-3 minutes until browned and tender but still crisp. Stir in spring onions and toss to mix well.

Add the cider vinegar, mustard, sugar and black pepper, tossing to coat vegetables. Pour over spinach leaves and turn leaves gently to coat; leaves will wilt at once. Serve immediately, garnished with slices of lemon and radish, if wished.

Serves 4-6.

BEAN STIR-FRY

175 g (6 oz) green beans, cut into 5 cm (2 in) pieces
175 g (6 oz) runner beans or flat beans, cut into 5 cm
   (2 in) pieces
175 g (6 oz) mange tout (snow peas) or sugar snap peas
115 ml (4 fl oz/½ cup) olive oil
1 onion, chopped
2 cloves garlic
430 g (15 oz) can red kidney beans, rinsed and drained
430 g (15 oz) can cannellini beans, rinsed and drained
350 g (12 oz) can sweetcorn, rinsed and drained
55 ml (2 fl oz/¼ cup) wine vinegar
3-6 teaspoons Dijon mustard
1 teaspoon sugar
225 g (8 oz) mature or medium Cheddar cheese, diced
3-4 tablespoons chopped fresh parsley

Half-fill the wok with water. Over high heat, bring to the boil. Add green beans and runner beans and simmer for 2 minutes. Add mange tout (snow peas) or sugar snap peas and bring back to the boil. Drain and rinse under cold running water. Wipe wok dry and return to heat. Heat the wok until hot. Add 2-3 tablespoons olive oil and swirl to coat wok. Add onion and garlic and stir-fry for 2-3 minutes until softened. Stir in kidney beans, cannellini beans and sweetcorn and stir-fry for 2-3 minutes.

Add reserved blanched beans and stir-fry for 3-4 minutes until heated through. Remove from heat, turn into a large bowl and cool slightly. In a small bowl, whisk the vinegar, mustard and sugar together. Whisk in the remaining olive oil and pour over warm bean mixture. Add the diced Cheddar cheese and parsley and toss to mix well. Serve warm or at room temperature.

Serves 6.

—————— PASTA PRIMAVERA ——————

450 g (1 lb) tagliatelle, linguine or thin spaghetti
2-4 tablespoons olive oil
225 g (8 oz) asparagus, cut into 5 cm (2 in) pieces
225 g (8 oz) broccoli florets, cut into small florets
2 yellow or green courgettes (zucchini), sliced
115 g (4 oz) mange tout (snow peas), cut in half if large
2-4 cloves garlic, finely chopped
400 g (14 oz) can chopped tomatoes
25 g (1 oz/2 tablespoons) butter
115 g (4 oz) frozen peas
4-6 tablespoons shredded fresh basil or
    chopped fresh dill
grated Parmesan, to serve

In the wok or a large saucepan, cook pasta according to packet directions.

Drain, turn into a large bowl, toss with 1 tablespoon olive oil and set aside. Heat the wok until hot. Add remaining oil and swirl to coat wok. Add asparagus and broccoli and stir-fry for 4-5 minutes until tender but still crisp. Remove to a bowl. Add courgettes (zucchini) and mange tout (snow peas) and stir-fry for 1-2 minutes until tender but still crisp. Remove to the bowl. Add garlic to oil remaining in wok and stir-fry for 1 minute. Stir in chopped tomatoes and their juice and simmer for 4-6 minutes until slightly thickened.

Stir butter into tomato sauce and add reserved vegetables, frozen peas, basil or dill and reserved pasta. Toss to coat well. Stir and toss for 2-3 minutes to heat through. Serve with grated Parmesan cheese.

Serves 4-6.

—PENNE, VODKA & TOMATOES—

450 g (1 lb) penne or rigatoni
2 tablespoons olive oil
1 onion, finely chopped
2 cloves garlic, finely chopped
400 g (14 oz) can plum tomatoes
½ teaspoon crushed dried chillies
115 g (4 oz) thinly sliced ham
115 ml (4 fl oz/½ cup) vodka
250 ml (9 fl oz/1 cup) whipping cream
55 g (2 oz/½ cup) Parmesan cheese, grated
4 tablespoons chopped fresh parsley
salt and freshly ground black pepper

Cook penne or rigatoni according to packet directions.

Drain and set aside. Heat the wok until hot. Add olive oil and swirl to coat wok. Add onion and garlic and stir-fry for 2 minutes until onion begins to soften. Add tomatoes and crushed chillies and bring to the boil. Reduce heat and simmer for 8-10 minutes until sauce thickens slightly.

Add ham and vodka and simmer for a further 5 minutes. Add cream and half the grated Parmesan and simmer for 3 minutes. Stir in penne or rigatoni and parsley and toss to coat pasta. Season with salt and pepper and cook for 1-2 minutes to heat through. Serve hot with the remaining Parmesan sprinkled over the top.

Serves 4-6.

Note: Garnish with extra parsley, if wished.

-MACARONI WITH AUBERGINES-

450 g (1 lb) aubergines (eggplants), cut into 0.5 cm
  (¼ in) matchstick strips
salt
450 g (1 lb) macaroni
3 tablespoons olive oil
3 cloves garlic, finely chopped
450 g (1 lb) plum or beefsteak tomatoes, peeled,
  seeded and chopped
1 fresh chilli, seeded and chopped
115 g (4 oz) Italian salami, cut into julienne strips
85 g (3 oz) black olives
2 tablespoons capers, rinsed and drained
4 tablespoons chopped fresh basil or oregano
115 g (4 oz) feta cheese, crumbled
25 g (1 oz/¼ cup) Parmesan cheese, grated
herb sprigs, to garnish

Place aubergine (eggplant) strips in a
colander and sprinkle with salt. Toss to mix,
then leave to stand, on a plate, for 1 hour.
Rinse under cold running water and pat dry
with absorbent kitchen paper. In a large
saucepan of boiling water, cook macaroni
according to packet directions. Drain and
set aside.

Heat wok until very hot. Add olive oil and
swirl to coat. Add aubergine (eggplant) and
stir-fry for 3-5 minutes until browned. Drain
on absorbent kitchen paper. Add garlic,
tomatoes and chilli and stir-fry for 2 minutes
until juices are absorbed. Add salami, olives,
capers, basil or oregano, aubergine (eggplant)
and macaroni and toss to coat well. Stir fry for
1-2 minutes to heat through. Add feta cheese
and toss. Sprinkle with Parmesan cheese,
garnish and serve hot.

Serves 6.

TORTELLONI SALAD

350 g (12 oz) green, cheese- or meat-filled tortelloni
115 ml (4 fl oz/½ cup) olive oil
2 cloves garlic, finely chopped
225 g (8 oz) asparagus, cut into 5 cm (2 in) pieces
175 g (6 oz) broccoli, cut into small flowerets
1 yellow pepper (capsicum), thinly sliced
175 g (6 oz) jar marinated artichoke hearts, drained
1 red onion, thinly sliced
2 tablespoons capers
3-4 tablespoons black olives
9 teaspoons red wine vinegar
3 teaspoons Dijon mustard
salt and freshly ground black pepper
3 tablespoons shredded fresh basil or parsley

In a large saucepan of boiling water, cook tortelloni according to packet directions. Drain and rinse. Drain again and toss with 1 tablespoon olive oil. Set aside. Heat wok until hot. Add 2 tablespoons olive oil to wok and swirl to coat. Add garlic, asparagus and broccoli and stir-fry for 4-5 minutes until vegetables are tender but still crisp. Add pepper (capsicum) and stir-fry for 1 minute. Remove vegetables to a large bowl and toss with reserved tortelloni, artichoke hearts, red onion, capers and olives. Allow to cool to room temperature.

In a small bowl, whisk together the wine vinegar, mustard, and salt and pepper to taste. Slowly whisk in remaining olive oil until creamy. Pour the dressing over the tortelloni and vegetables. Add the shredded basil or parsley and toss gently to mix well. Serve at room temperature.

Serves 4-6.

—PASTA WITH PEANUT SAUCE—

450 g (1 lb) thin spaghetti or egg noodles
2 tablespoons sesame oil
225 g (8 oz) lean minced pork
1 red pepper (capsicum), thinly sliced
115 g (4 oz) mange tout (snow peas), cut in
    half diagonally
1 tablespoon sugar
2.5 cm (1 in) piece fresh root ginger, grated
½ teaspoon crushed dried chillies
55 ml (2 fl oz/¼ cup) soy sauce
9 teaspoons cider vinegar
150 ml (5 fl oz/⅔ cup) peanut butter
8 spring onions, thinly sliced
2 tablespoons chopped fresh coriander
coriander sprigs, to garnish

In a large saucepan of boiling water, cook spaghetti or egg noodles according to packet directions. Drain and toss with 1 tablespoon sesame oil. Set aside. Place minced pork in a cold wok and cook over moderate heat, stirring and breaking up large pieces until pork is no longer pink. Add red pepper (capsicum), mange tout (snow peas) and sugar and stir-fry for 1 minute. Add ginger, chillies, soy sauce, vinegar, peanut butter and 150 ml (5 fl oz/ ⅔ cup) hot water, stirring until sauce bubbles and peanut butter thins out. Add a little more water if necessary.

Stir in spring onions and reserved spaghetti. Toss and stir-fry for 2-3 minutes until spaghetti is coated evenly with sauce and heated through. Sprinkle with chopped coriander and remaining sesame oil and toss. Serve hot, garnished with sprigs of coriander.

Serves 4-6.

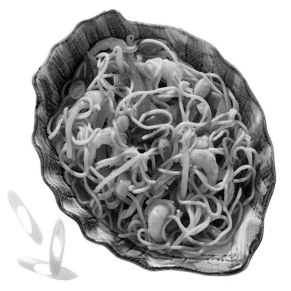

——— SINGAPORE NOODLES ———

225 g (8 oz) thin round egg noodles
55 ml (2 fl oz/¼ cup) vegetable oil
2 cloves garlic, chopped
2.5 cm (1 in) piece fresh root ginger, peeled and
    finely chopped
1 fresh chilli, seeded and chopped
1 red pepper (capsicum), thinly sliced
115 g (4 oz) mange tout (snow peas), sliced if large
4-6 spring onions, finely sliced
175 g (6 oz) peeled cooked prawns, defrosted if
    frozen
115 g (4 oz) beansprouts, trimmed, rinsed and dried
70 ml (2½ fl oz/⅓ cup) tomato ketchup (sauce)
1 teaspoon chilli powder
1-2 teaspoons chilli sauce

In a large saucepan of boiling water, cook the
noodles according to packet directions.
Drain and toss with 1 tablespoon of the oil.
Set aside. Heat the wok until hot. Add
remaining oil and swirl to coat the wok. Add
garlic, ginger and chilli and stir-fry for 1
minute. Add red pepper (capsicum) and
mange tout (snow peas) and stir-fry for
1 minute.

Add spring onions, prawns and beansprouts
and stir in the tomato ketchup (sauce), chilli
powder, chilli sauce and 115 ml (4 fl oz/
½ cup) water. Bring to the boil. Add noodles
and toss. Stir-fry for 1-2 minutes until coated
with sauce and heated through. Turn into
large shallow serving bowl and serve at once.

Serves 4.

COCONUT NOODLES

225 g (8 oz) wholewheat linguine, tagliatelle
    or spaghetti
55 ml (2 fl oz/¼ cup) groundnut oil
115 g (4 oz) shiitake or oyster mushrooms
1 red pepper (capsicum), thinly sliced
½ small Chinese cabbage, thinly shredded
115 g (4 oz) mange tout (snow peas), thinly sliced
4-6 spring onions, thinly sliced
175 ml (6 fl oz/¾ cup) unsweetened coconut milk
2 tablespoons rice wine or dry sherry
1 tablespoon soy sauce
1 tablespoon oyster sauce
1 teaspoon Chinese chilli sauce
3 teaspoons cornflour dissolved in 2 tablespoons water
8 tablespoons chopped fresh mint or coriander
mint or coriander sprigs, to garnish

In a large saucepan of boiling water, cook the
noodles according to the packet directions.
Drain and toss with 1 tablespoon of groundnut oil. Heat the wok until hot. Add the
remaining oil and swirl to coat wok. Add
mushrooms, pepper (capsicum) and Chinese
cabbage and stir-fry for 2-3 minutes until
vegetables begin to soften. Stir in reserved
noodles, mange tout (snow peas) and spring
onions and stir-fry for 1 minute to combine.

Slowly pour in coconut milk, rice wine or
sherry, soy sauce, oyster sauce and chilli
sauce and bring to simmering point. Stir the
cornflour mixture and, pushing ingredients
to one side, stir into the wok. Stir to combine
liquid ingredients well, then stir in chopped
mint or coriander and toss to coat well. Stir-
fry for 2-3 minutes until heated through.
Serve hot, garnished with sprigs of mint
or coriander.

Serves 4.

COLD SPICY NOODLES

450 g (1 lb) soba (buckwheat) noodles or
  wholewheat spaghetti
2 tablespoons sesame oil
2 cloves garlic, finely chopped
1 green pepper (capsicum), thinly sliced
115 g (4 oz) mange tout (snow peas), sliced
115 g (4 oz) daikon (mooli), thinly sliced
2 tablespoons light soy sauce
3 teaspoons cider vinegar
3-6 teaspoons Chinese chilli paste or sauce
2 teaspoons sugar
70 ml (2½ fl oz/⅓ cup) peanut butter or sesame paste
8-10 spring onions, thinly sliced
toasted chopped peanuts or toasted sesame seeds,
  to garnish
cucumber matchsticks, to serve (optional)

In a large saucepan of boiling water, cook
noodles or spaghetti according to packet
directions. Drain and rinse well. Drain again
and toss with 1 tablespoon sesame oil. Set
aside. Heat the wok until very hot. Add
remaining sesame oil and swirl to coat. Add
garlic and stir-fry for 5-10 seconds. Add pepper (capsicum), mange tout (snow peas) and
daikon. Stir-fry for 1 minute until fragrant
and brightly coloured.

Stir in soy sauce, vinegar, chilli paste or
sauce, sugar, peanut butter or sesame paste
and 55 ml (2 fl oz/¼ cup) hot water. Remove
from heat. Stir until peanut butter or sesame
paste is diluted and smooth, adding a little
more water, if necessary. Add reserved
noodles and toss to coat. Turn into a large
shallow bowl and allow to cool. Before
serving, toss again, adding spring onions and
sprinkling with peanuts or sesame seeds.
Serve with cucumber, if wished.

Serves 4-6.

THAI RICE NOODLES

225 g (8 oz) flat rice noodles
3 tablespoons vegetable oil
2 cloves garlic, peeled and chopped
1 red pepper (capsicum), thinly sliced
1 tablespoon soy sauce
1 teaspoon chilli sauce
6 teaspoons nam pla (fish sauce)
4 teaspoons wine vinegar
1 tablespoon brown sugar
450 g (1 lb) cooked peeled prawns, defrosted if frozen
    and patted dry
175 g (6 oz) beansprouts, trimmed and rinsed
6 spring onions, thinly sliced
4 tablespoons sesame oil
3 tablespoons chopped peanuts, to garnish

Place the rice noodles in a large, heatproof
bowl. Pour over enough hot water to cover
noodles by 5 cm (2 in) and leave to stand for
15-20 minutes until softened. Drain and set
aside. Heat the wok until hot. Add the oil
and swirl to coat wok. Add garlic and red
pepper (capsicum) and stir-fry for 2-3 minutes
until pepper is tender but still crisp. Add
noodles, soy sauce, chilli sauce, nam pla (fish
sauce), vinegar and brown sugar and stir-fry
for 1 minute. Add a little water if noodles
begin to stick.

Stir in prawns, beansprouts, spring onions
and sesame oil and stir-fry for 2-3 minutes
until prawns are heated through. Sprinkle
with peanuts and serve hot.

Serves 4.

──── ASIAN-STYLE FRIED RICE ────

250 g (9 oz/1½ cups) long-grain rice
2 tablespoons vegetable oil
2 cloves garlic, finely chopped
1 fresh red chilli, seeded and chopped
1 cm (½ in) piece fresh root ginger, peeled and minced
2 tablespoons light soy sauce
1 teaspoon sugar
2 teaspoons nam pla (fish sauce)
½ teaspoon turmeric
4-6 spring onions, thinly sliced
450 g (1 lb) cooked peeled small prawns
225 g (8 oz) can unsweetened pineapple chunks,
   juice reserved
3-4 tablespoons chopped fresh coriander

In a large saucepan of boiling water, cook the rice for 15-17 minutes until just tender. Drain in a colander and rinse under cold running water until cold. Set aside. Heat the wok until hot. Add vegetable oil and swirl to coat wok. Add garlic, chilli and ginger and stir-fry for 1 minute. Add soy sauce, sugar, nam pla (fish sauce), turmeric and spring onions, stirring to dissolve sugar.

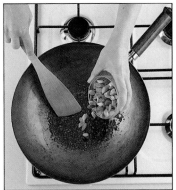

Stir in reserved rice, prawns and pineapple chunks, tossing to mix. Stir-fry for 3-4 minutes until rice is heated through, adding a little reserved pineapple juice if rice begins to stick. Stir in coriander, turn into serving bowl and serve at once.

Serves 4-6.

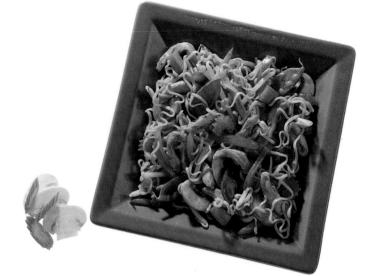

CHOW MIEN

3 tablespoons soy sauce
2 tablespoons dry sherry or rice wine
1 teaspoon Chinese chilli paste or sauce
1 tablespoon sesame oil
6 teaspoons cornflour
350 g (12 oz) skinned and boned chicken breasts,
    cut into shreds
225 g (8 oz) Chinese long egg noodles or linguine
2 tablespoons vegetable oil
2 stalks celery, thinly sliced
175 g (6 oz) mushrooms
1 red or green pepper (capsicum), thinly sliced
115 g (4 oz) mange tout (snow peas)
4-6 spring onions
115 ml (4 fl oz/½ cup) chicken stock or water
115 g (4 oz) beansprouts, trimmed and rinsed

In a shallow baking dish, combine the soy
sauce, sherry or rice wine, chilli paste or
sauce, sesame oil and cornflour. Add the
shredded chicken and toss to coat evenly.
Allow to stand 20 minutes. In a large saucepan of boiling water, cook the egg noodles or
linguine according to the packet directions.
Drain and set aside.

Heat wok until hot. Add oil and swirl to coat
wok. Add celery, mushrooms and pepper.
Stir-fry for 2-3 minutes until vegetables begin
to soften. Add mange tout and spring onions
and stir-fry for 1 minute. Remove to a bowl.
Add chicken and marinade to wok. Stir-fry
for 2-3 minutes until chicken is cooked. Add
stock, bring to the boil, then add noodles or
linguine and reserved vegetables and beansprouts. Toss and stir-fry for 1-2 minutes until
sauce thickens and noodles are hot.

Serves 4-6.

WOK-STYLE PAELLA

2 tablespoons olive oil
450 g (1 lb) Spanish chorizo sausage or hot,
   Italian- style sausage, cut into 2.5 cm (1 in) slices
450 g (1 lb) skinned and boned chicken breasts,
   cut into 2.5 cm (1 in) strips
1 onion, chopped
2-3 cloves garlic, finely chopped
1 green or red pepper (capsicum), diced
400 g (14 oz) can Italian-style tomatoes
450 g (1 lb/2⅔ cups) long-grain rice
½ teaspoon crushed dried chillies
½ teaspoon dried thyme
1 teaspoon crushed saffron threads
225 g (8 oz) green beans, cut into 2.5 cm (1 in) pieces
225 g (8 oz) cooked peeled prawns (optional)
parsley sprigs and lime or lemon wedges, to garnish

Heat wok until hot. Add oil and swirl to coat wok. Add chorizo or Italian sausage and stir-fry for 4-5 minutes until golden. Remove to a plate. Add chicken pieces to oil in wok and stir-fry for 3-4 minutes until golden. Remove to the plate.

Add onion, garlic and pepper to wok. Stir-fry for 3-4 minutes. Add tomatoes, rice, 450 ml (16 fl oz/2 cups) water, chillies, thyme and saffron. Boil, add the sausage and reduce heat to low. Cover wok and cook gently for 20-30 minutes until rice is tender. Add chicken and green beans. Cook, covered, for 5-7 minutes more. Add prawns and fluff with a fork. Cook, uncovered, for 2-3 minutes. Garnish and serve.

Serves 6-8.

—BANANAS WITH RUM & LIME—

55 g (2 oz/4 tablespoons) butter
55 g (2 oz/¼ cup) light brown sugar
½ teaspoon ground cinnamon
4 bananas, peeled and cut diagonally into 1 cm (½ in)
    slices
70 ml (2½ fl oz/⅓ cup) light rum
grated rind and juice of 1 lime or lemon
2 tablespoons chopped almonds, toasted
shavings of fresh coconut or toasted shredded coconut,
    to garnish (optional)

Heat the wok until hot. Add the butter and
swirl to melt and coat wok. Stir in sugar and
cinnamon and cook for 1 minute until sugar
melts and mixture bubbles.

Add banana slices and stir-fry gently for 1-2
minutes, tossing to coat all pieces and heat
through. Add rum and, with a match, light
rum to ignite. Shake wok gently until flames
subside.

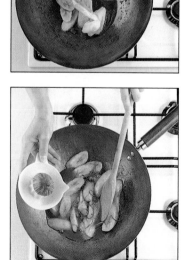

Add rind and juice of the lime or lemon and
toasted almonds, and stir in gently. Spoon
into dessert dishes and garnish with fresh or
toasted coconut.

Serves 4.

── TOFFEE PEARS & PECANS ──

4 dessert pears, cut lengthwise in half and cored
6 teaspoons lemon juice
70 g (2½ oz/5 tablespoons) butter
70 g (2½ oz/about ½ cup packed) brown sugar
1 teaspoon ground cinnamon
½ teaspoon ground ginger
85 g (3 oz/1 cup) pecan halves
250 ml (9 fl oz/1 cup) double (heavy) or
    whipping cream
few drops vanilla essence

Cut pear halves into 0.5 cm (¼ in) thick slices. Sprinkle with the lemon juice.

Heat the wok until hot. Add 2 tablespoons butter and 3 tablespoons brown sugar and swirl to melt and coat wok. Stir until sugar melts and bubbles. Add pear slices, cinnamon, ginger and pecans and stir-fry gently for 4-6 minutes until pear slices are tender but still crisp. Remove pear slices and pecans to a shallow serving bowl.

Add remaining butter and sugar and stir for 2 minutes until sugar dissolves and sauce boils and bubbles. Stir in cream and bring to the boil. Simmer for 2-3 minutes until sauce thickens. Remove from heat, stir in vanilla essence and pour over pear slices and pecans. Cool slightly before serving or serve at room temperature.

Serves 4-6.

— STIR-FRIED GINGERED FRUITS —

225 g (8 oz) fresh raspberries
1-2 tablespoons sugar
3 teaspoons lemon juice
3-6 teaspoons framboise
45 g (1½ oz/3 tablespoons) butter
450 g (1 lb) peaches or nectarines, stoned and sliced
175 g (6 oz) apricots, stoned and sliced
2-3 yellow or red plums, stoned and sliced
225 g (8 oz) black cherries, stoned
225 g (8 oz) seedless green grapes
2 tablespoons stem ginger in syrup or crystallized
    ginger, chopped
½ teaspoon ground ginger
115 g (4 oz) blueberries
mint, to garnish
yogurt or sour cream, to serve (optional)

In a blender or food processor, purée raspberries with sugar and lemon juice. Strain through a sieve into a small bowl to remove seeds. Stir in framboise and a little water if necessary to thin the sauce. Chill until ready to serve. Heat the wok until hot. Add butter and swirl to melt and coat wok. Add peach or nectarine, apricot and plum slices and stir-fry gently for 3-4 minutes until fruit just begins to soften.

Add cherries, grapes, stem or crystallized ginger and ground ginger. Stir-fry for 2-3 minutes more until sliced fruits are tender and cherries and grapes just heated through. Remove wok from heat and stir in blueberries. Arrange fruits on a shallow serving dish and cool slightly. Drizzle with a little raspberry sauce and pass remaining sauce separately. Garnish with mint and, if you like, serve with yogurt or sour cream.

Serves 6-8.

MAPLE-GLAZED APPLES

1 lemon
4 dessert apples, cut lengthwise in half and cored
55 g (2 oz/4 tablespoons) butter
1 ½ tablespoons light brown sugar
2-3 tablespoons maple syrup
1 teaspoon ground cinnamon
double (heavy) cream, to serve (optional)

With a swivel-bladed vegetable peeler, remove rind from lemon and cut into julienne strips.

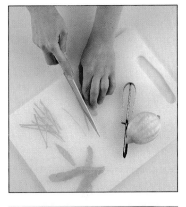

Squeeze juice from lemon. Cut apple halves into 1 cm (½ in) slices and sprinkle with the lemon juice. Heat the wok until hot. Add butter, sugar, maple syrup and cinnamon and swirl and stir until sugar melts and sauce bubbles.

Add apple slices and lemon juice and the julienne strips of rind. Stir-fry gently for 3-5 minutes until apple slices just begin to feel tender and are well glazed. Spoon into dessert dishes and, if you like, drizzle with a little cream. Serve warm.

Serves 4-6.

INDEX